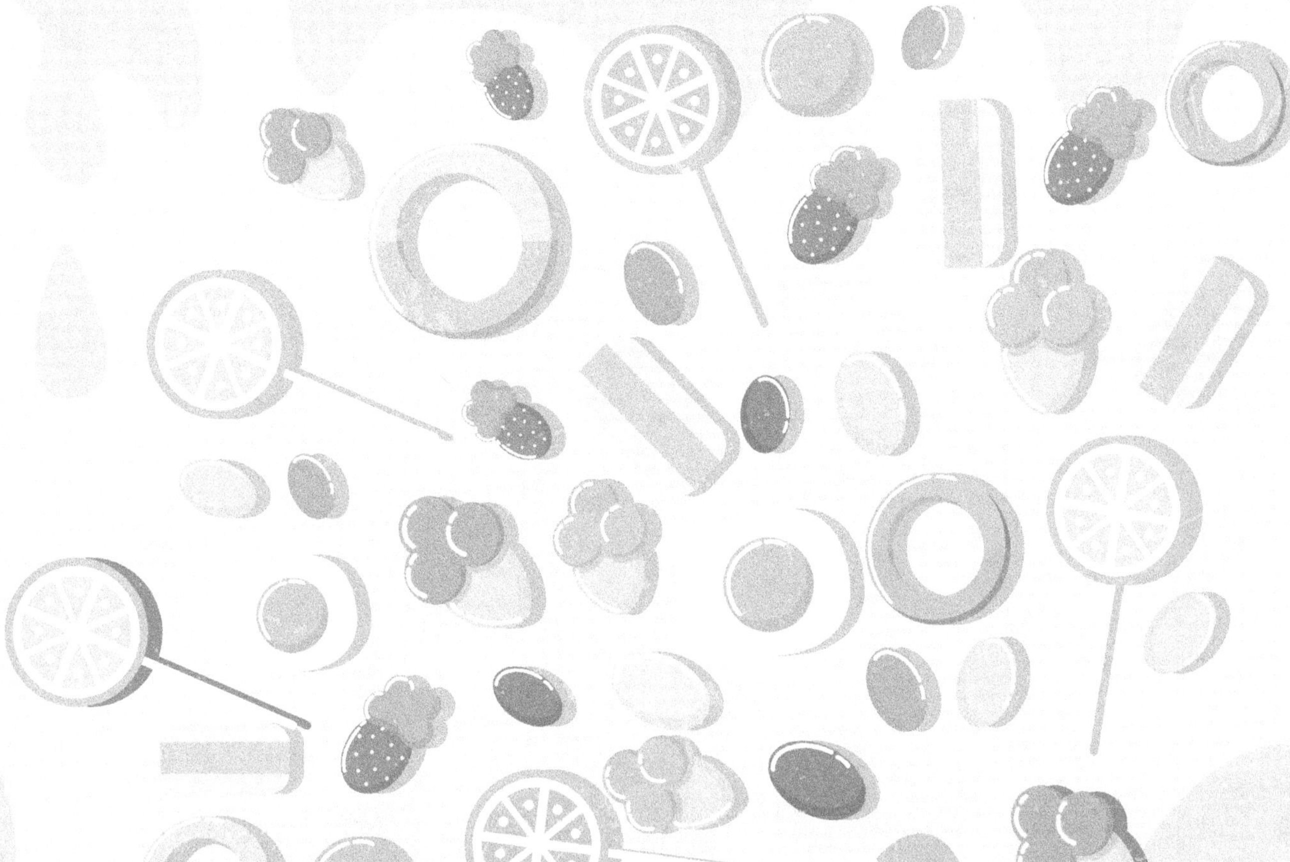

THIS BOOK BELONGS TO

...... ...... ...... ...... ...... ...... ...... ......

...... ...... ...... ...... ...... ...... ...... ......

...... ...... ...... ...... ...... ...... ...... ......

# Color Test

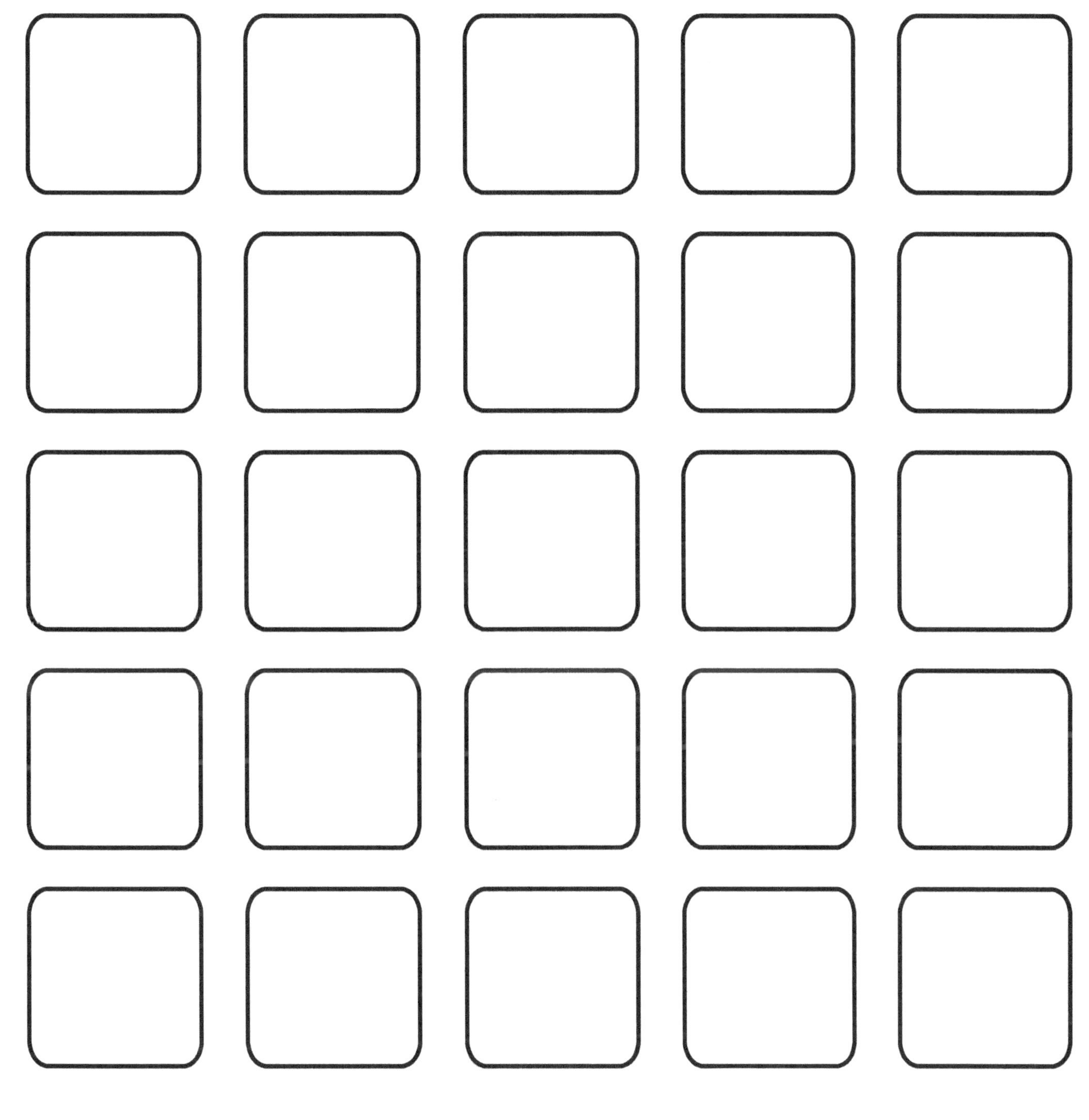

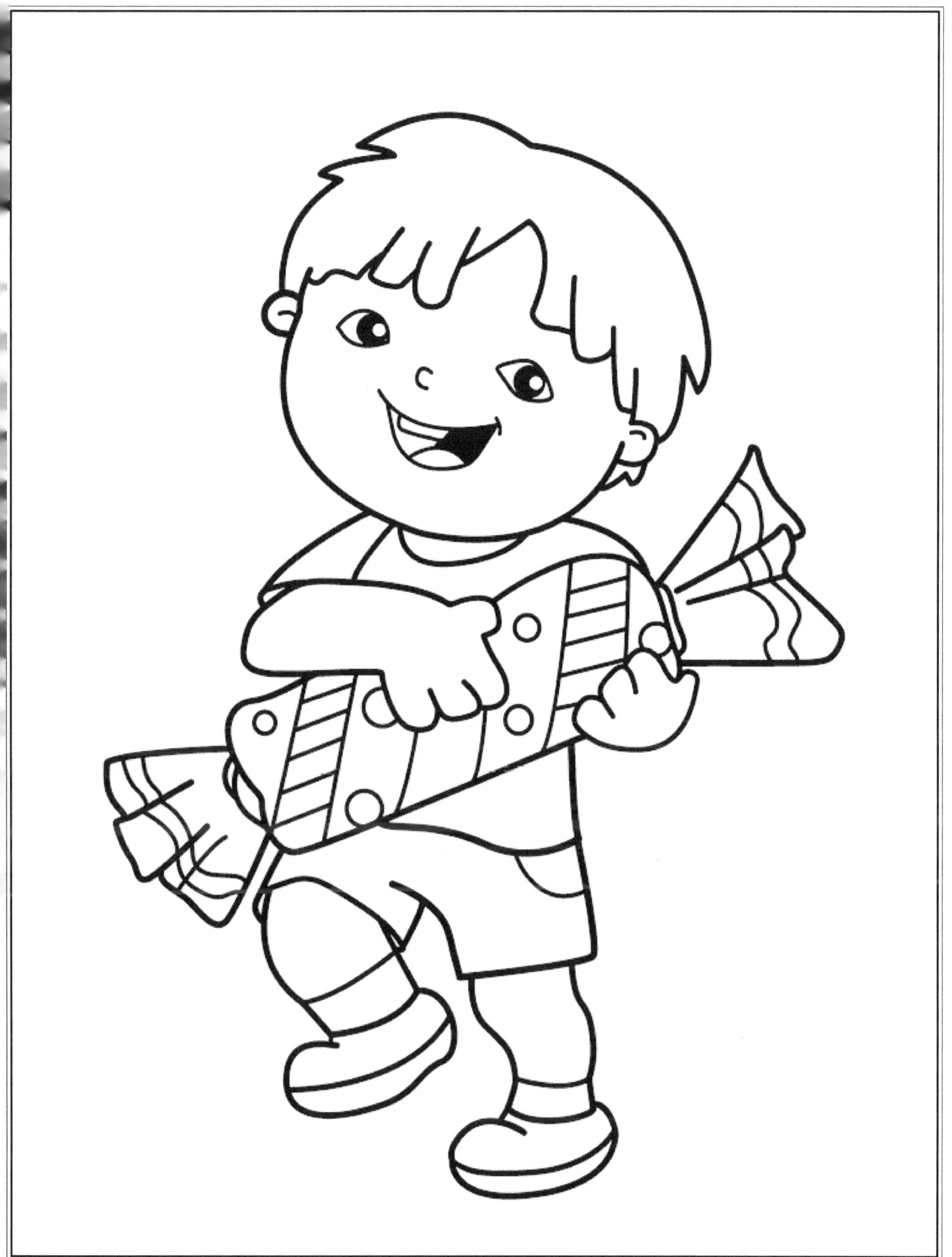

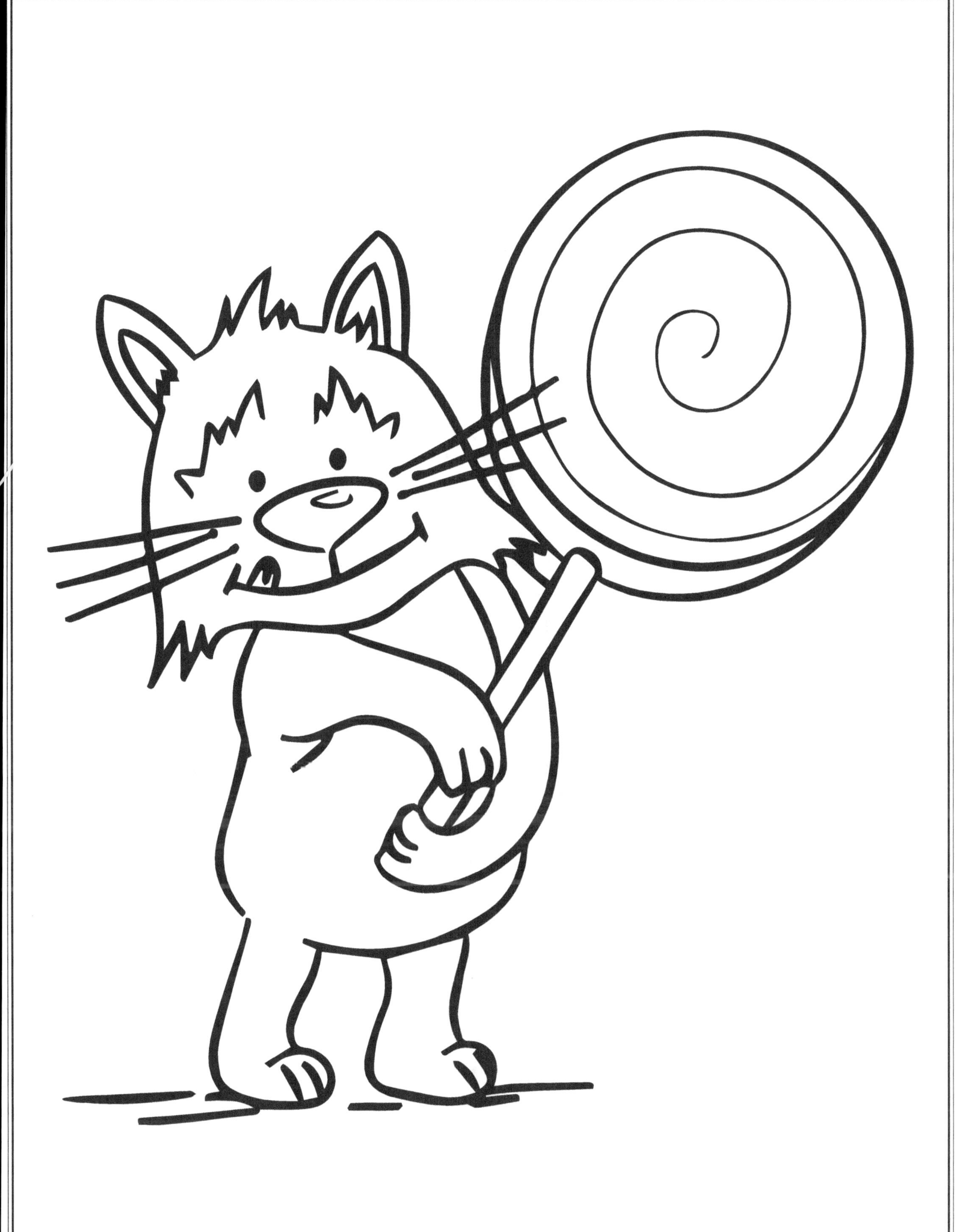

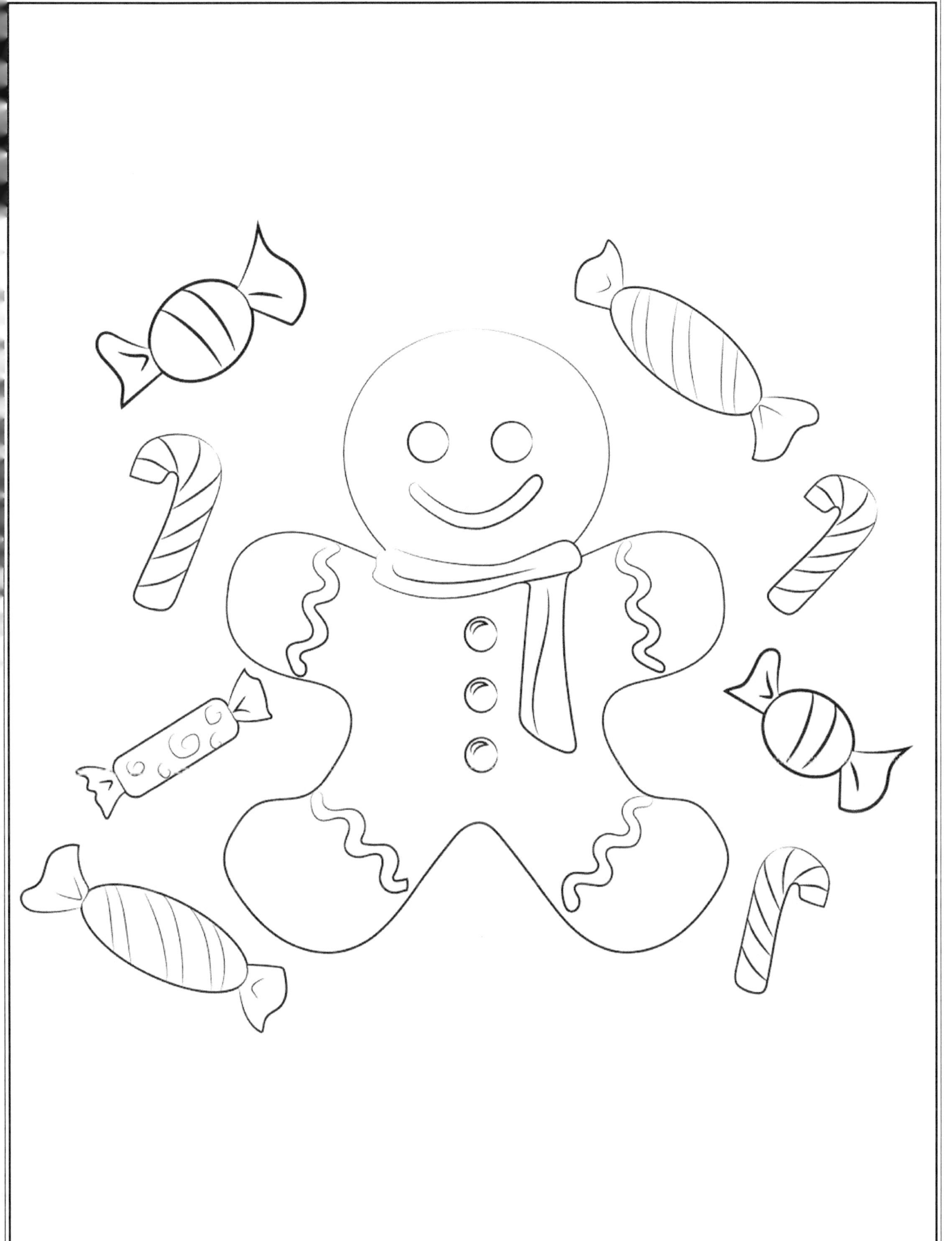

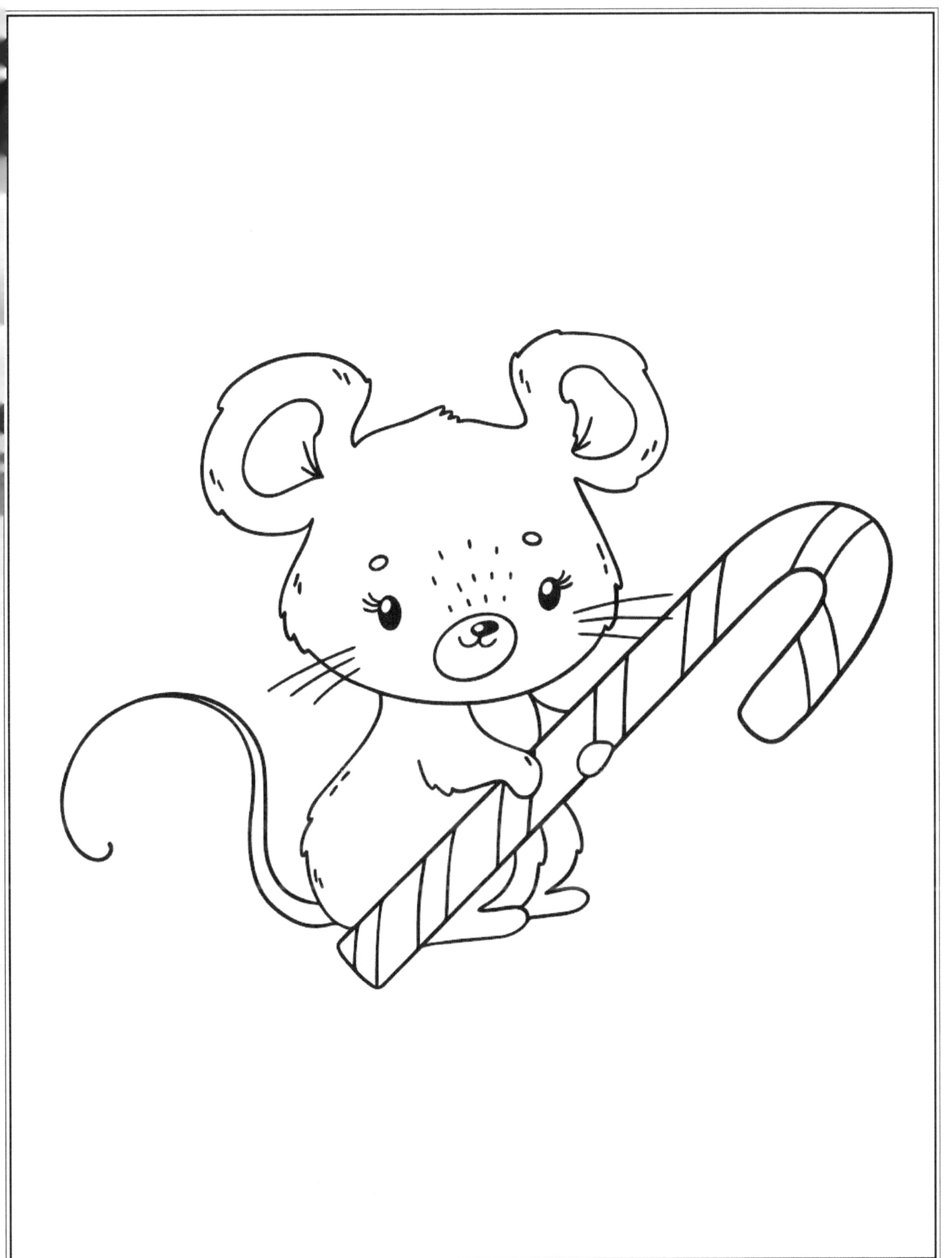

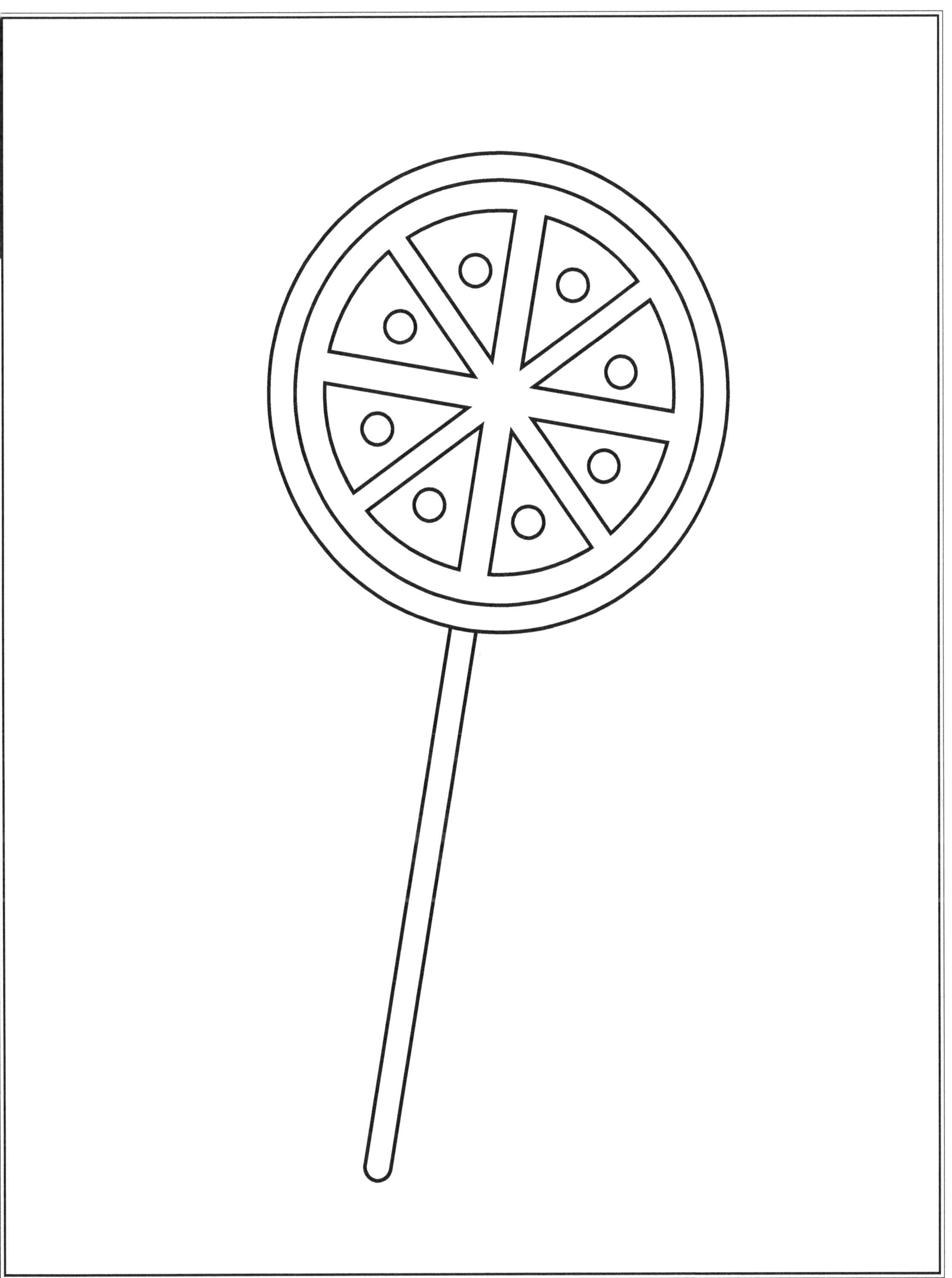

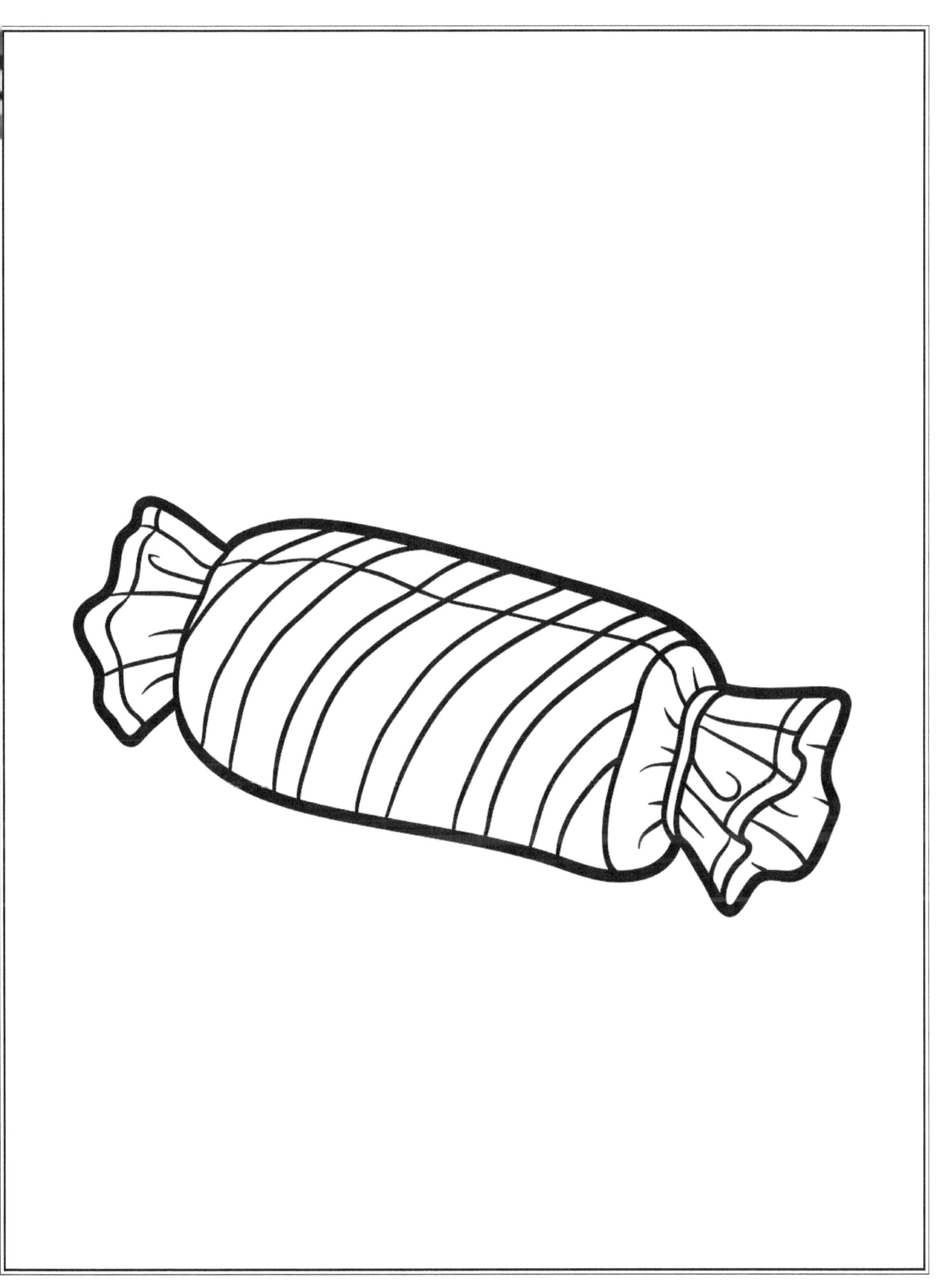

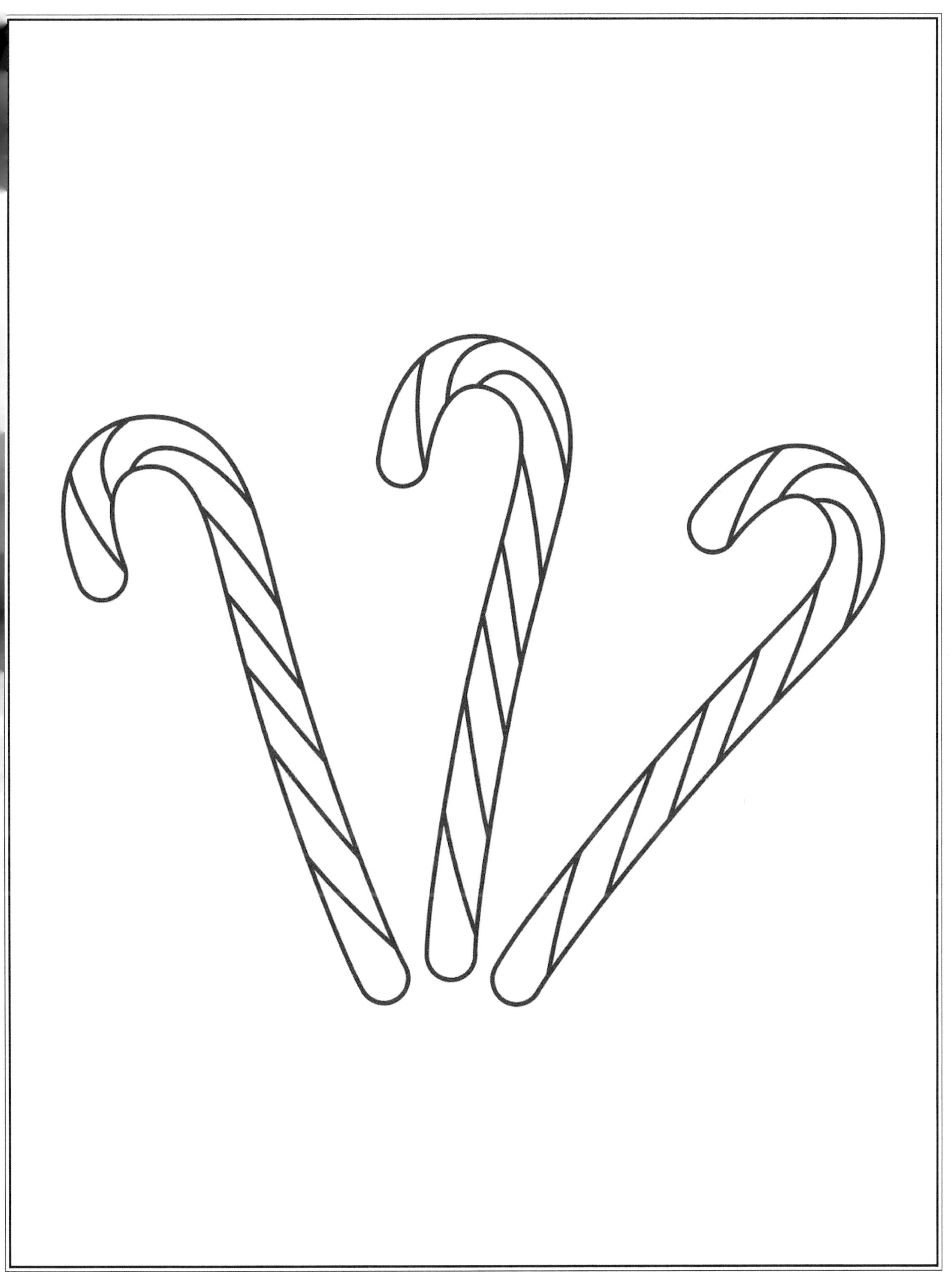

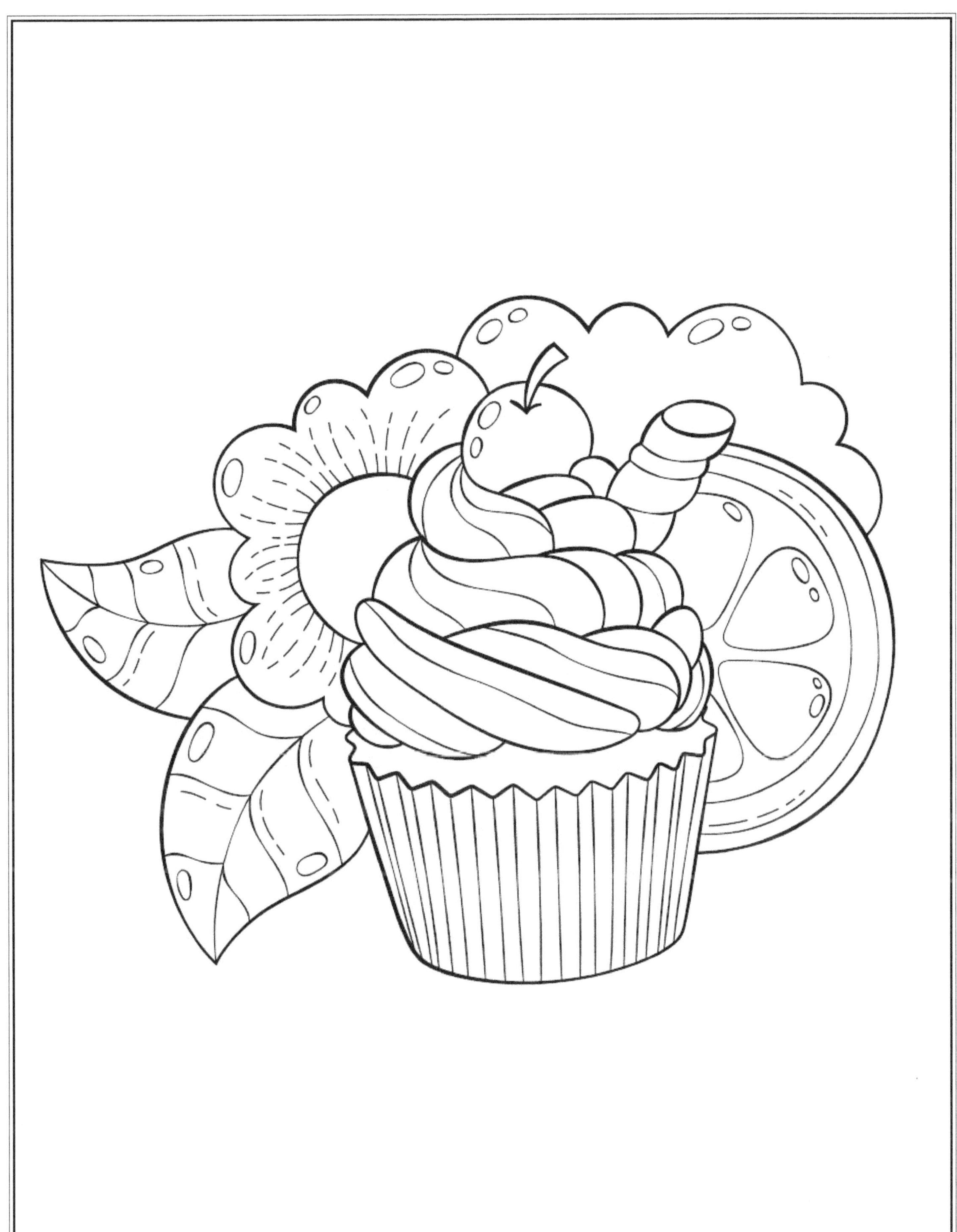

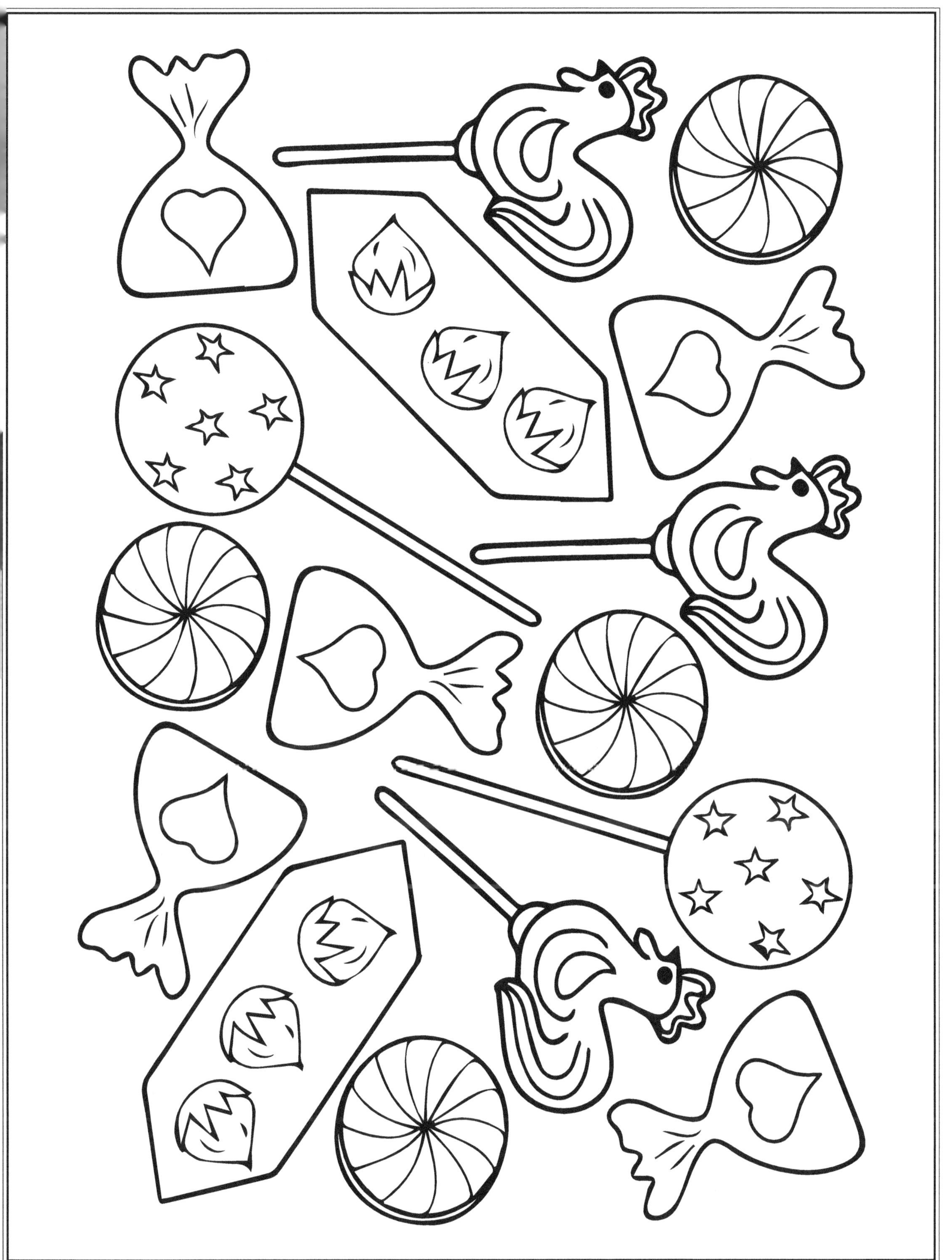

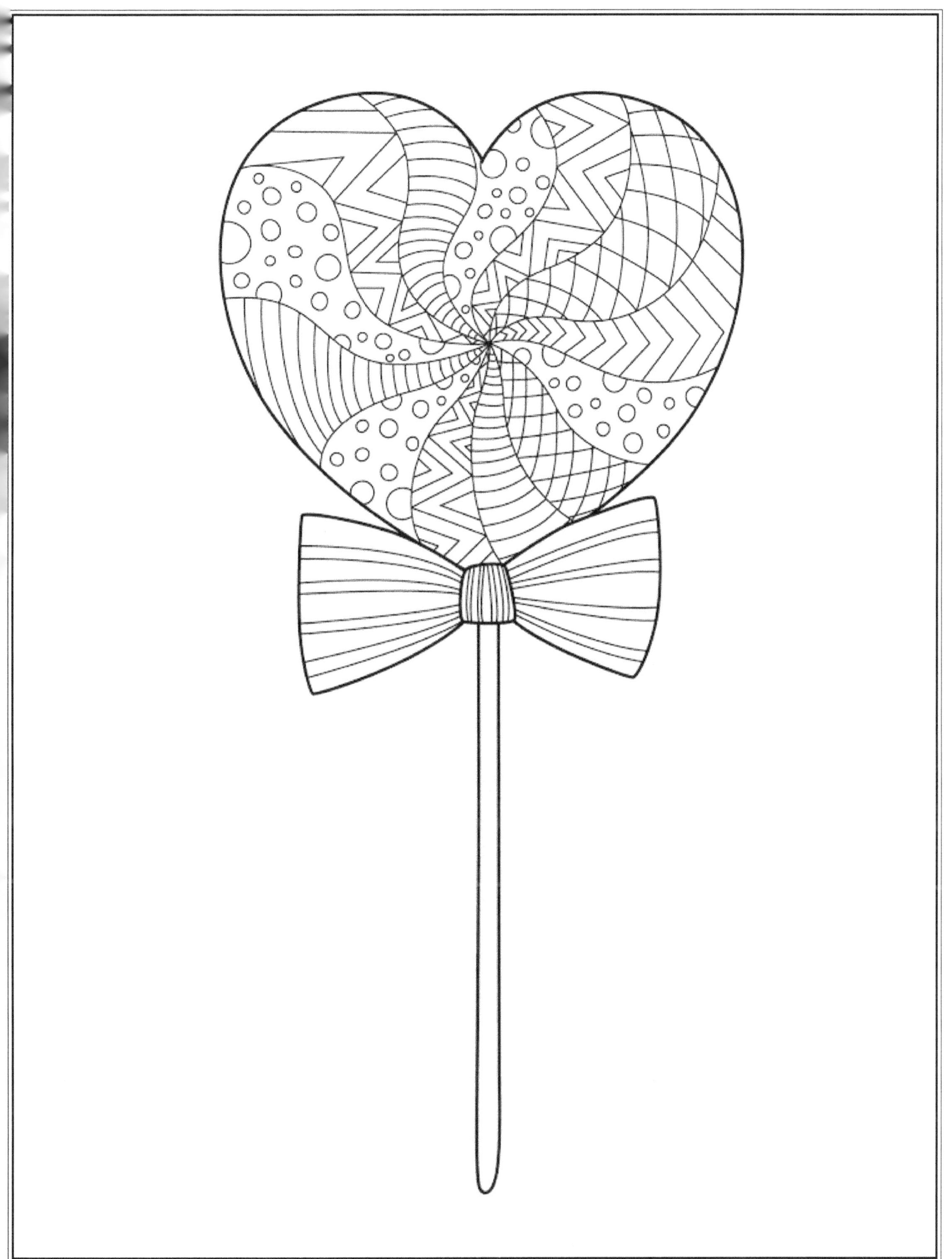

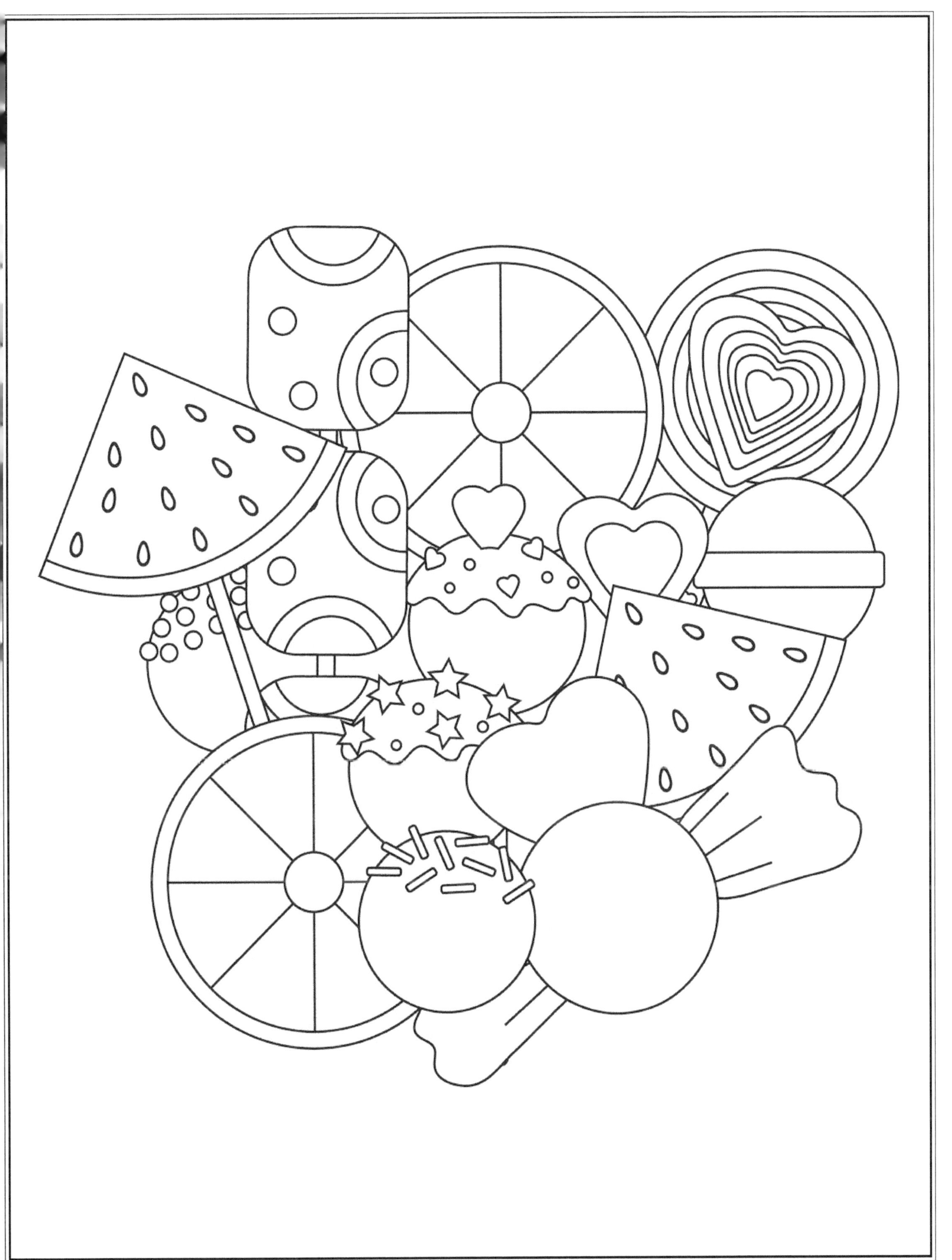

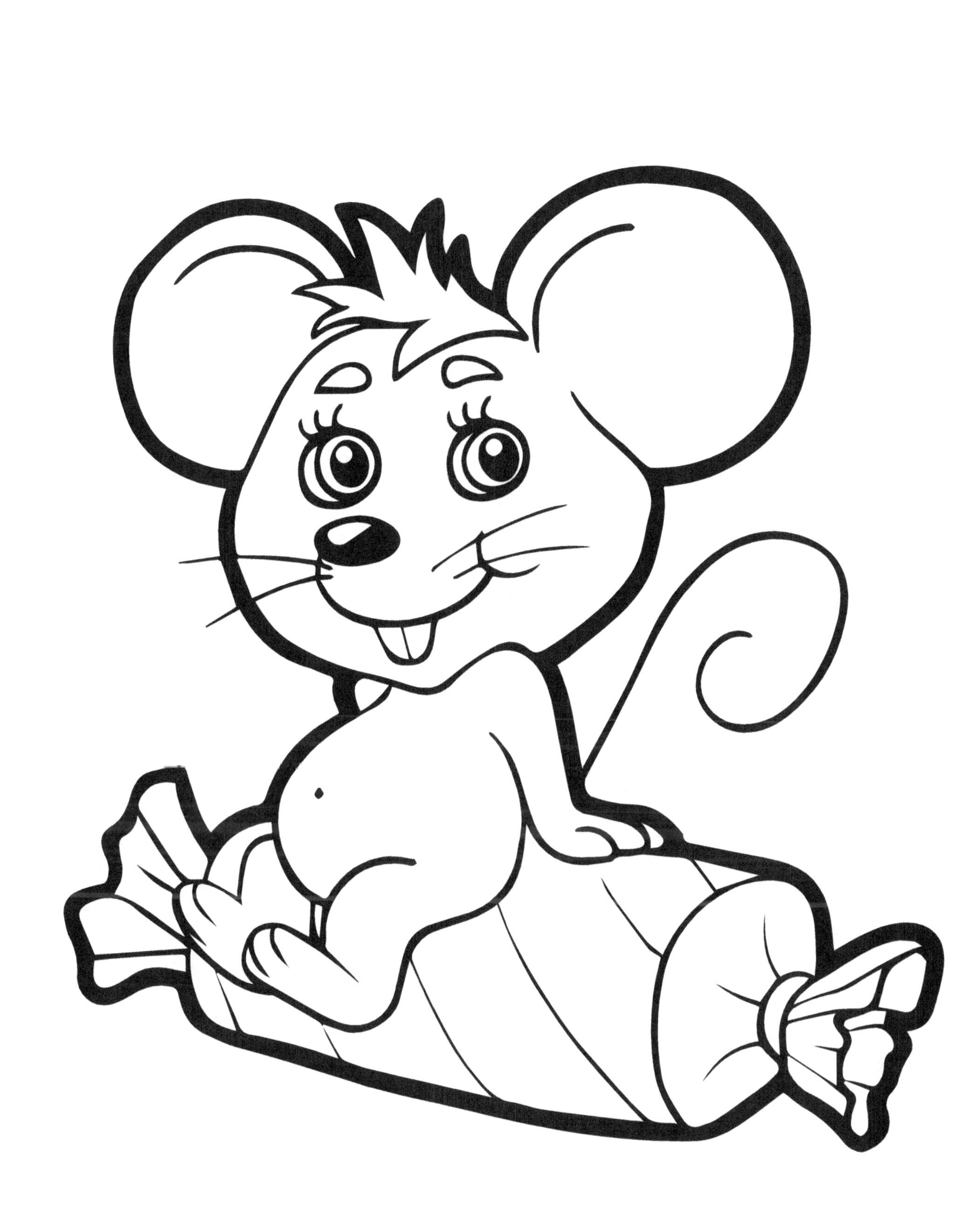

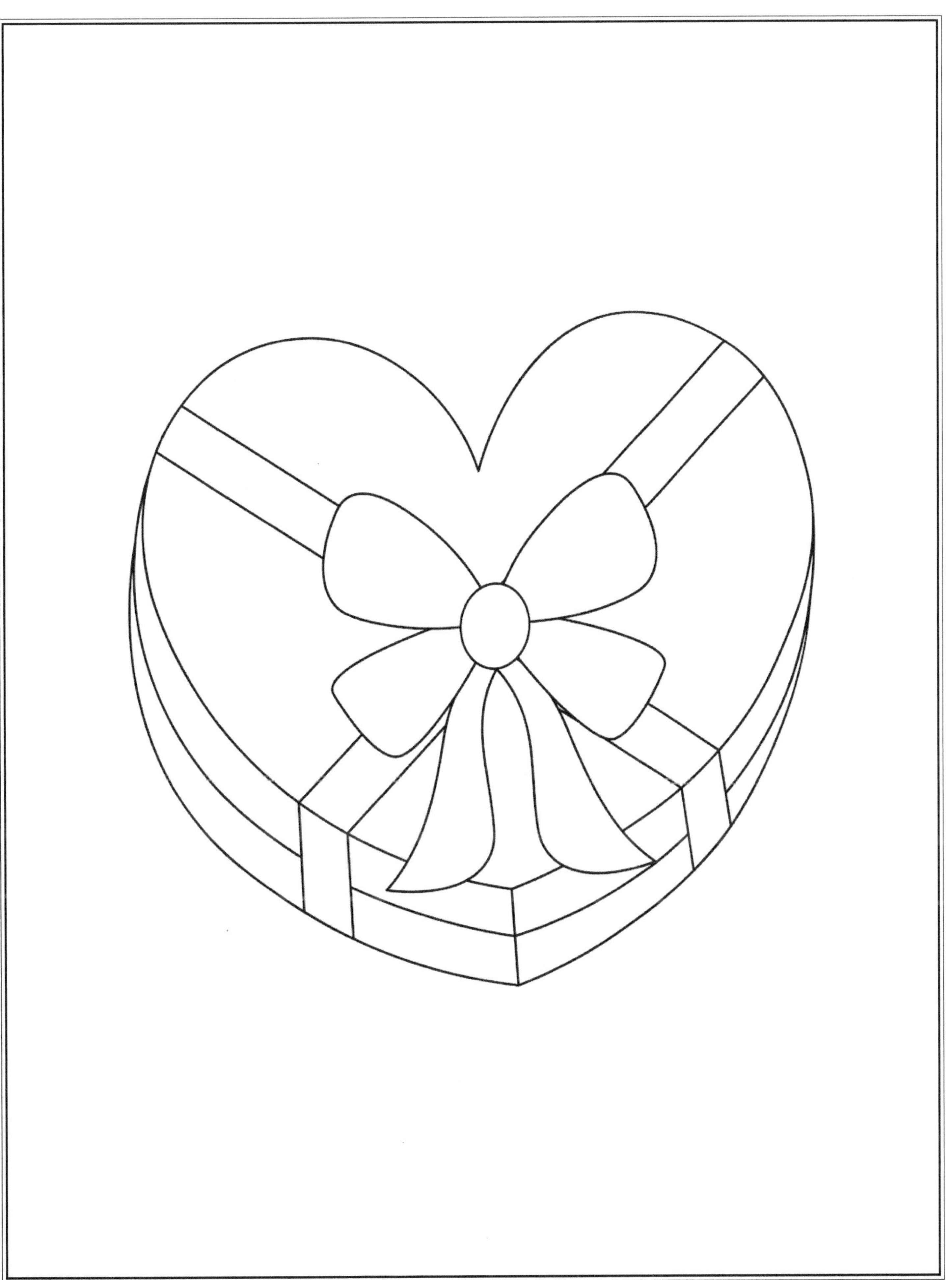

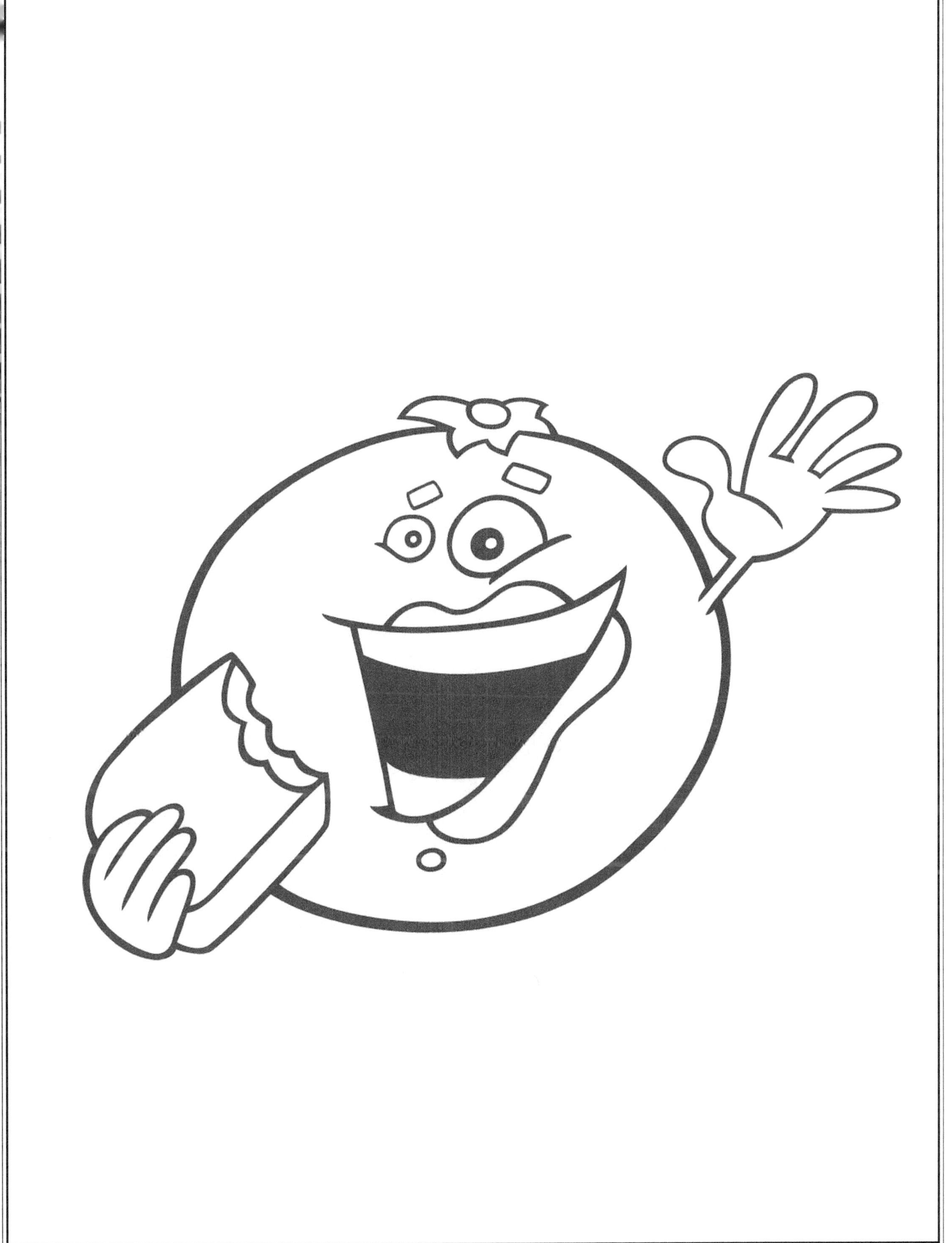

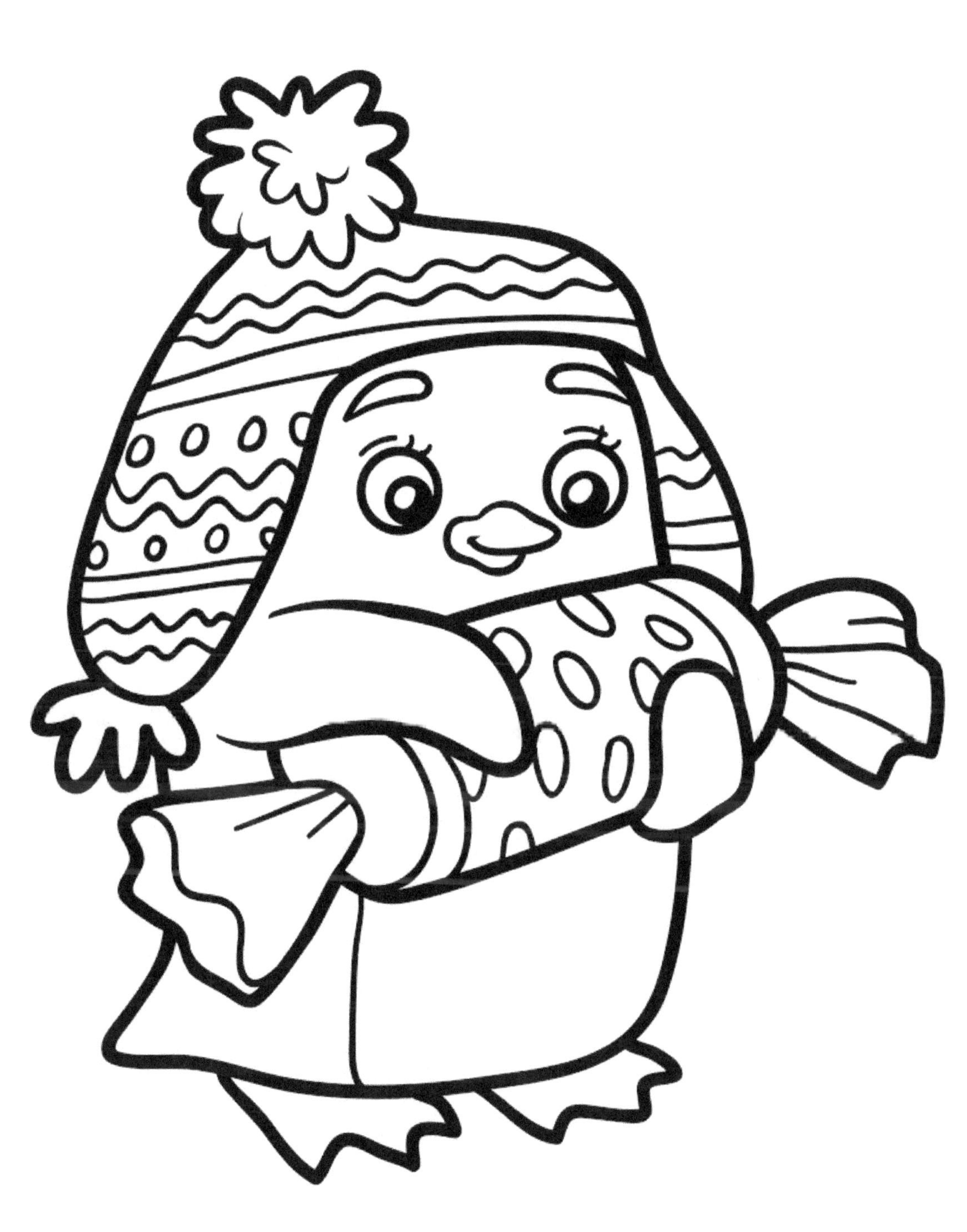

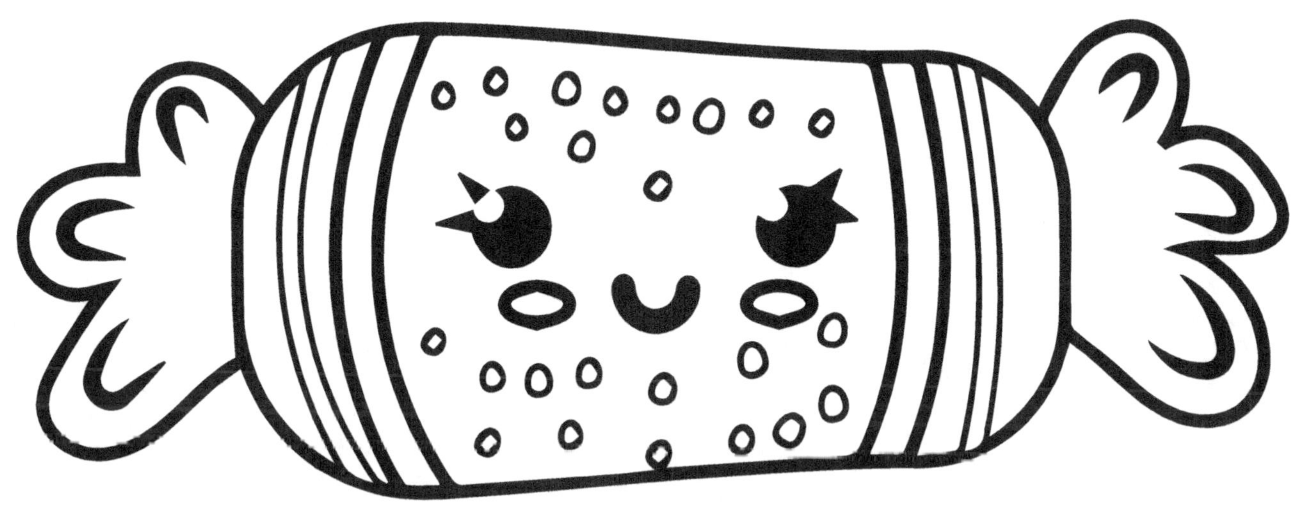

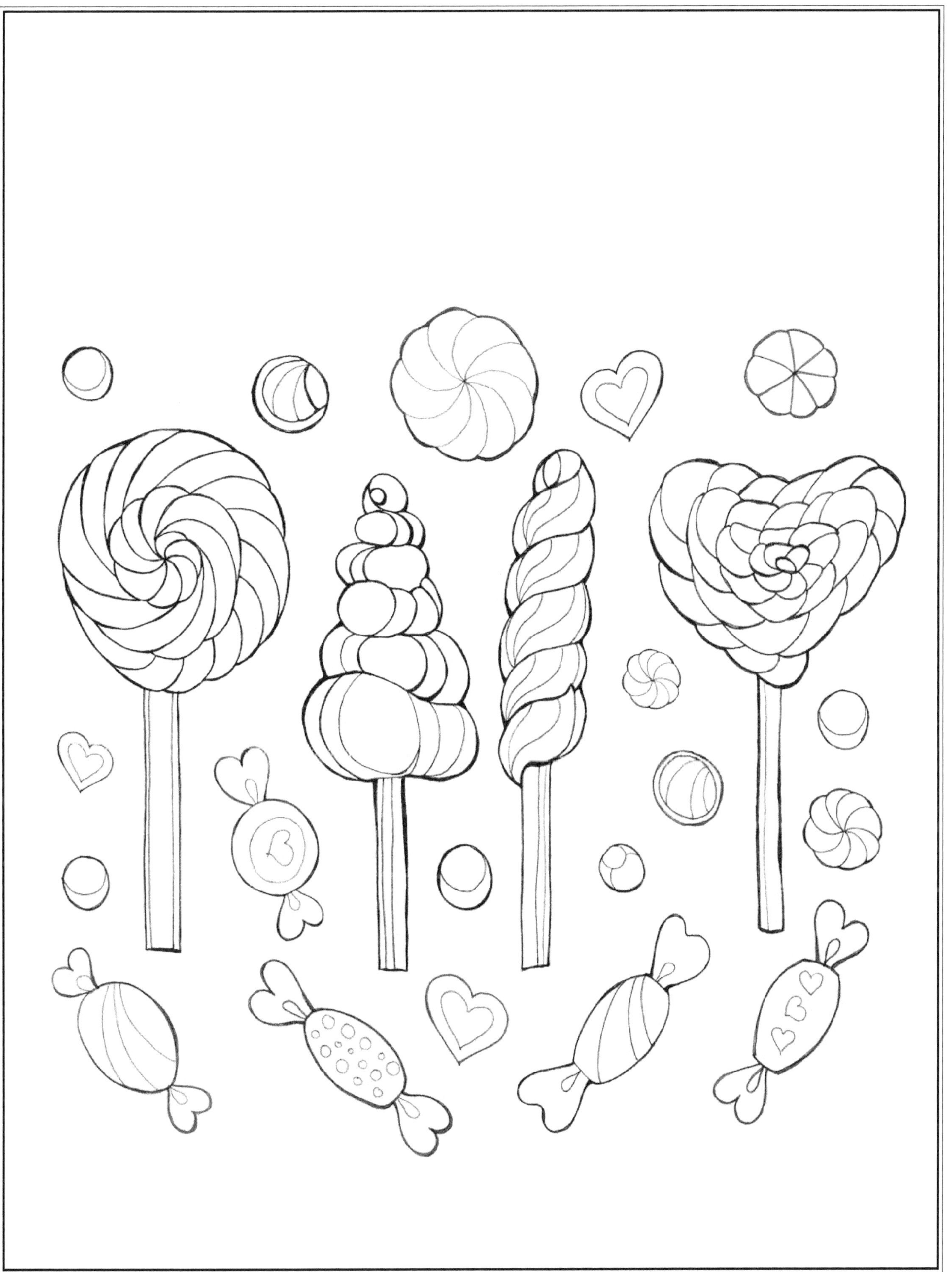

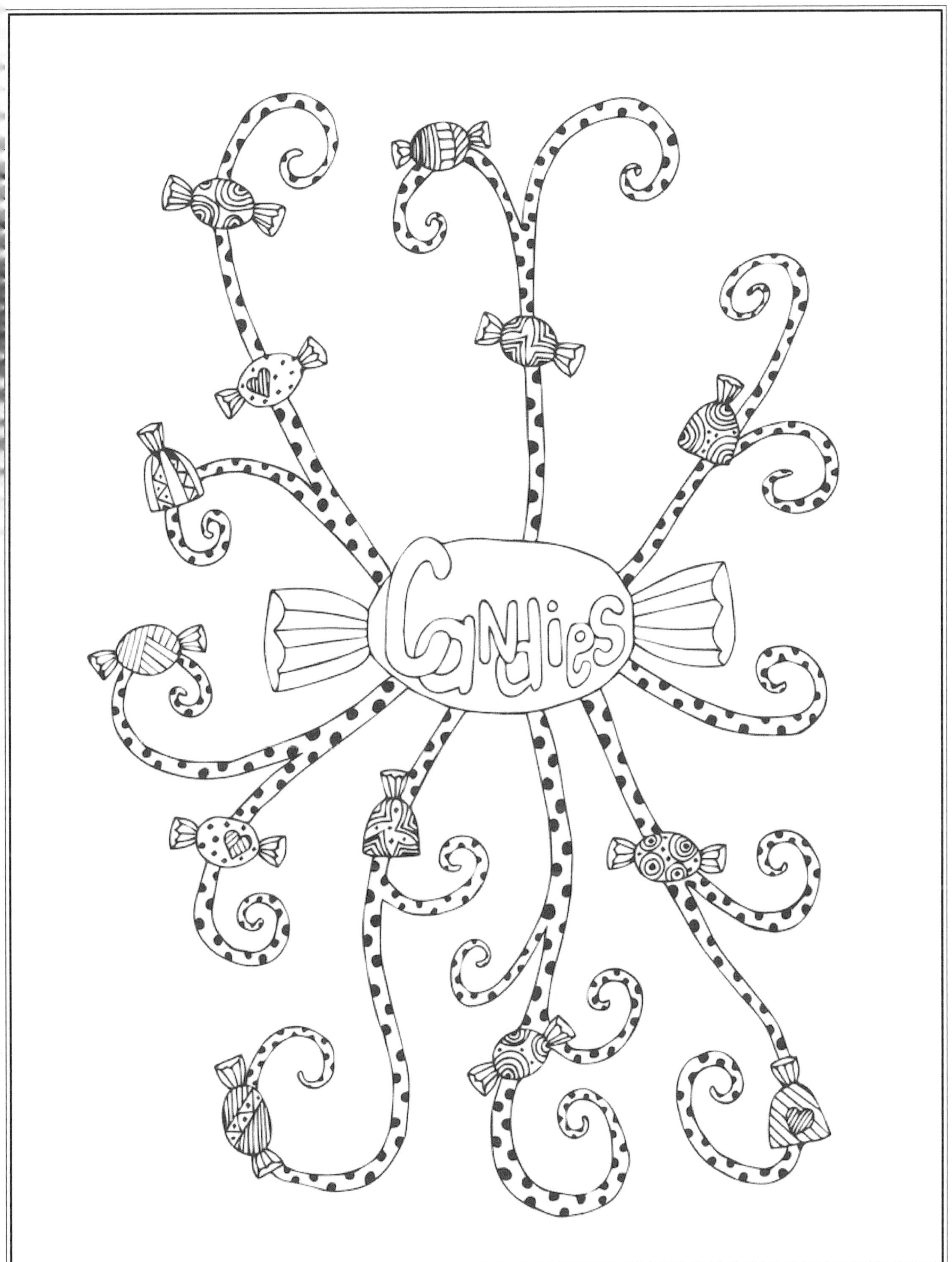
Candies

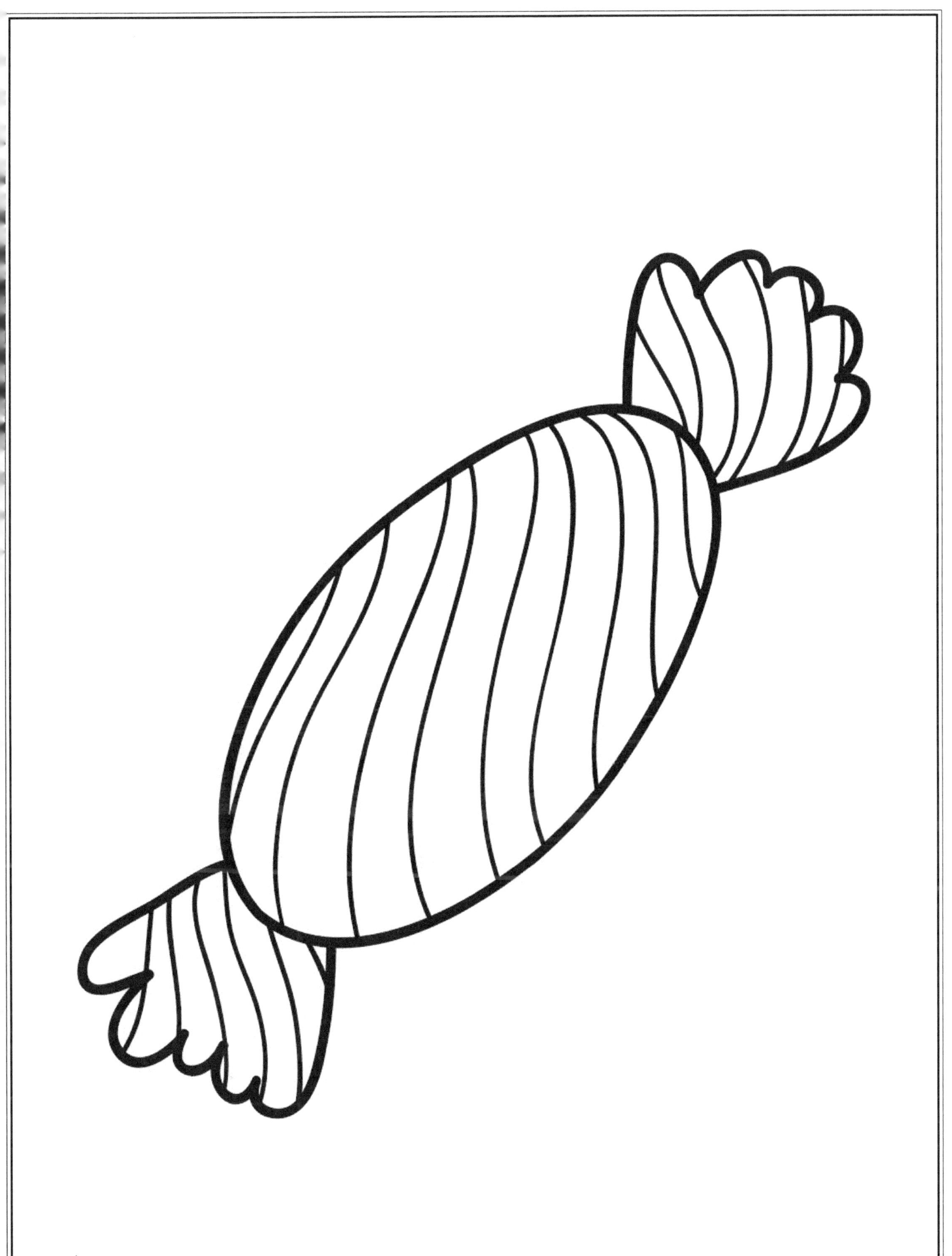

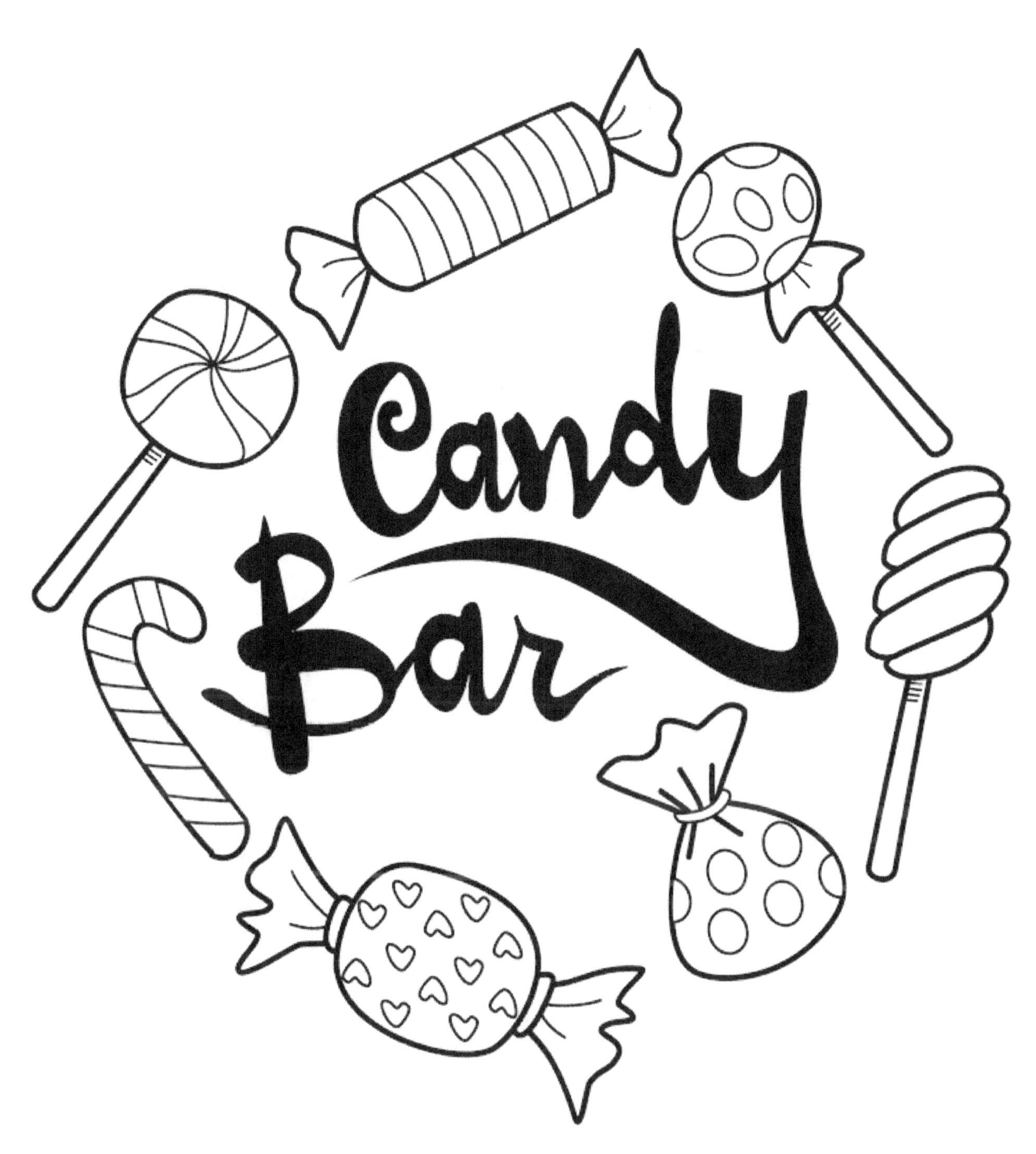
Candy
Bar

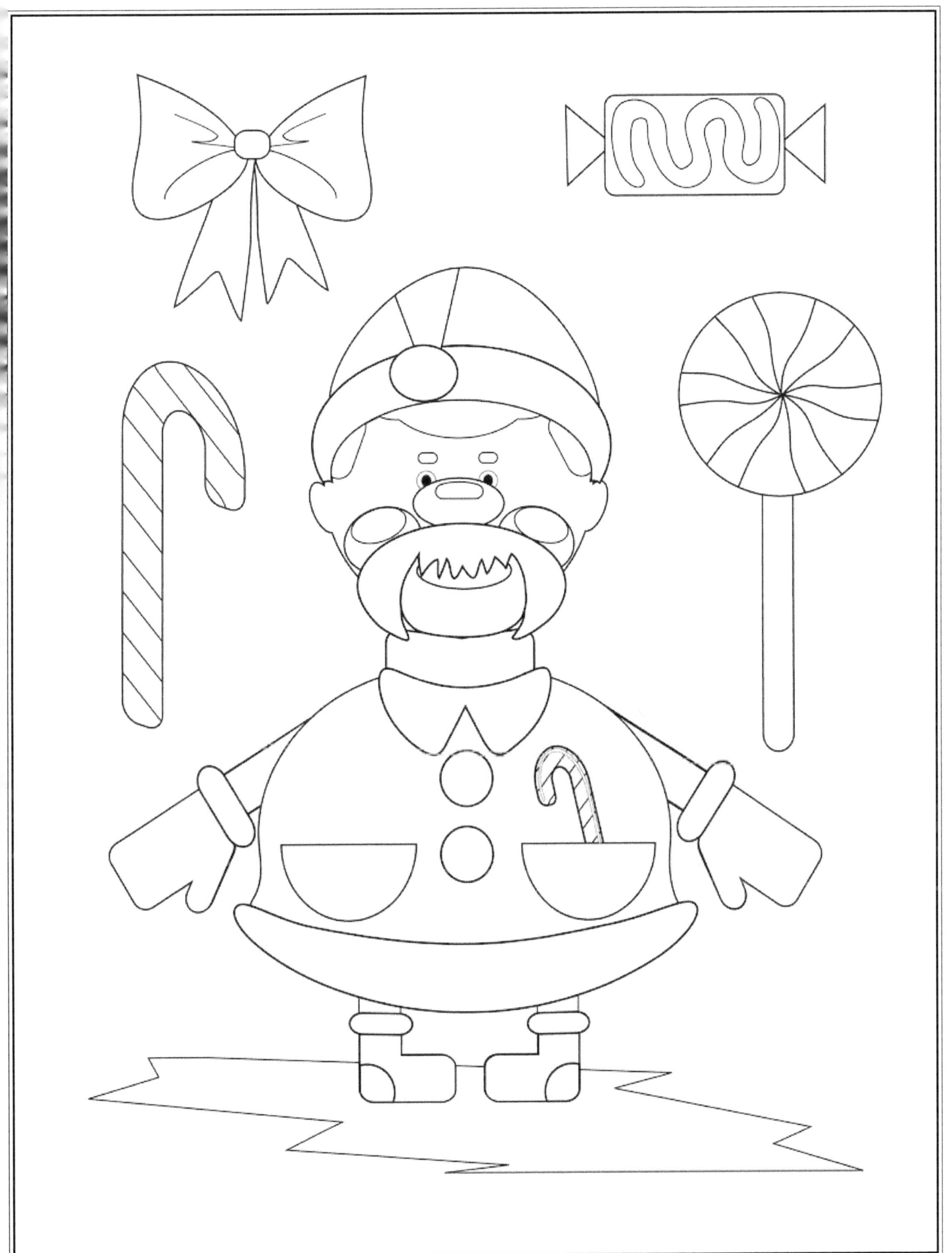

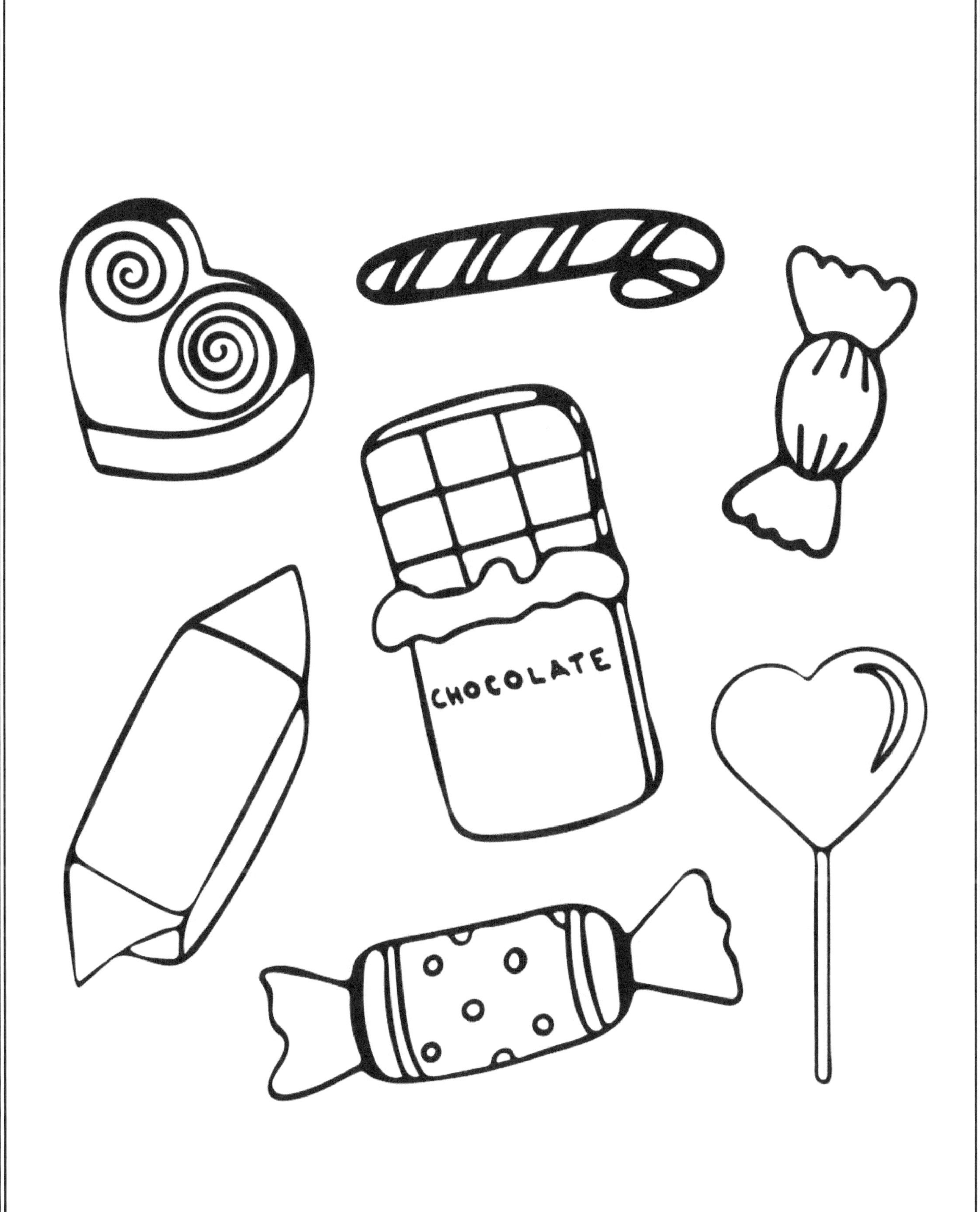
CHOCOLATE

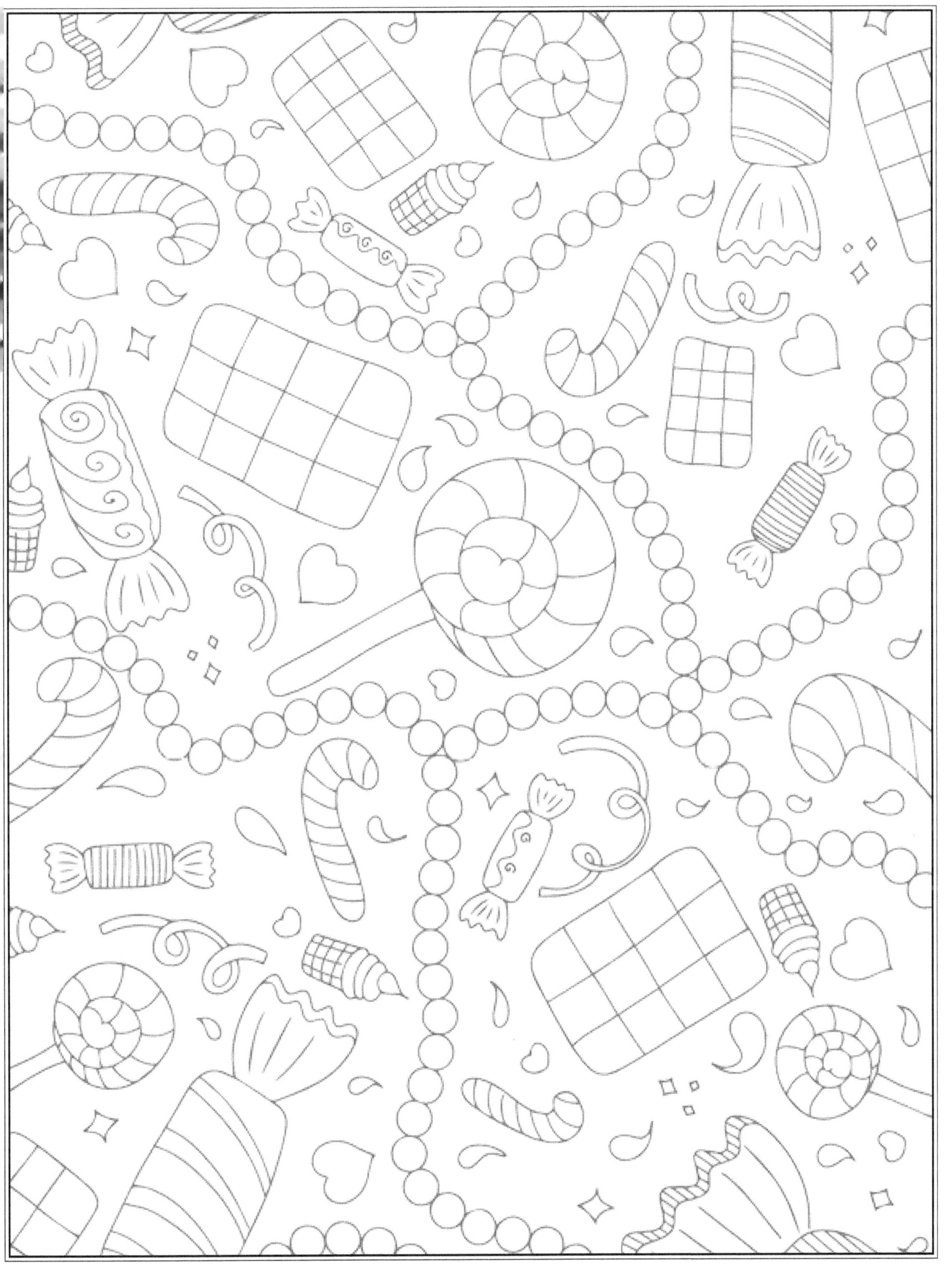

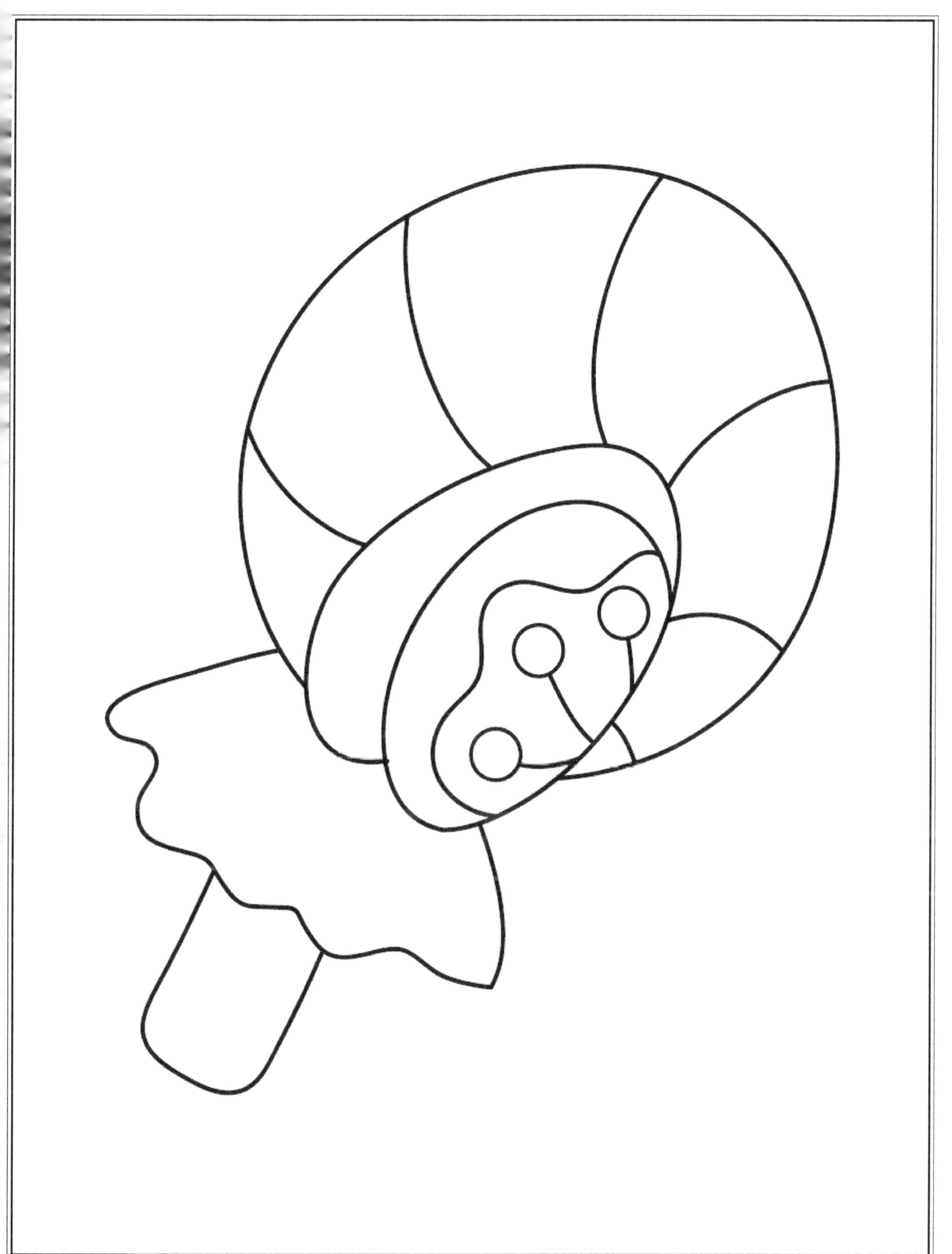

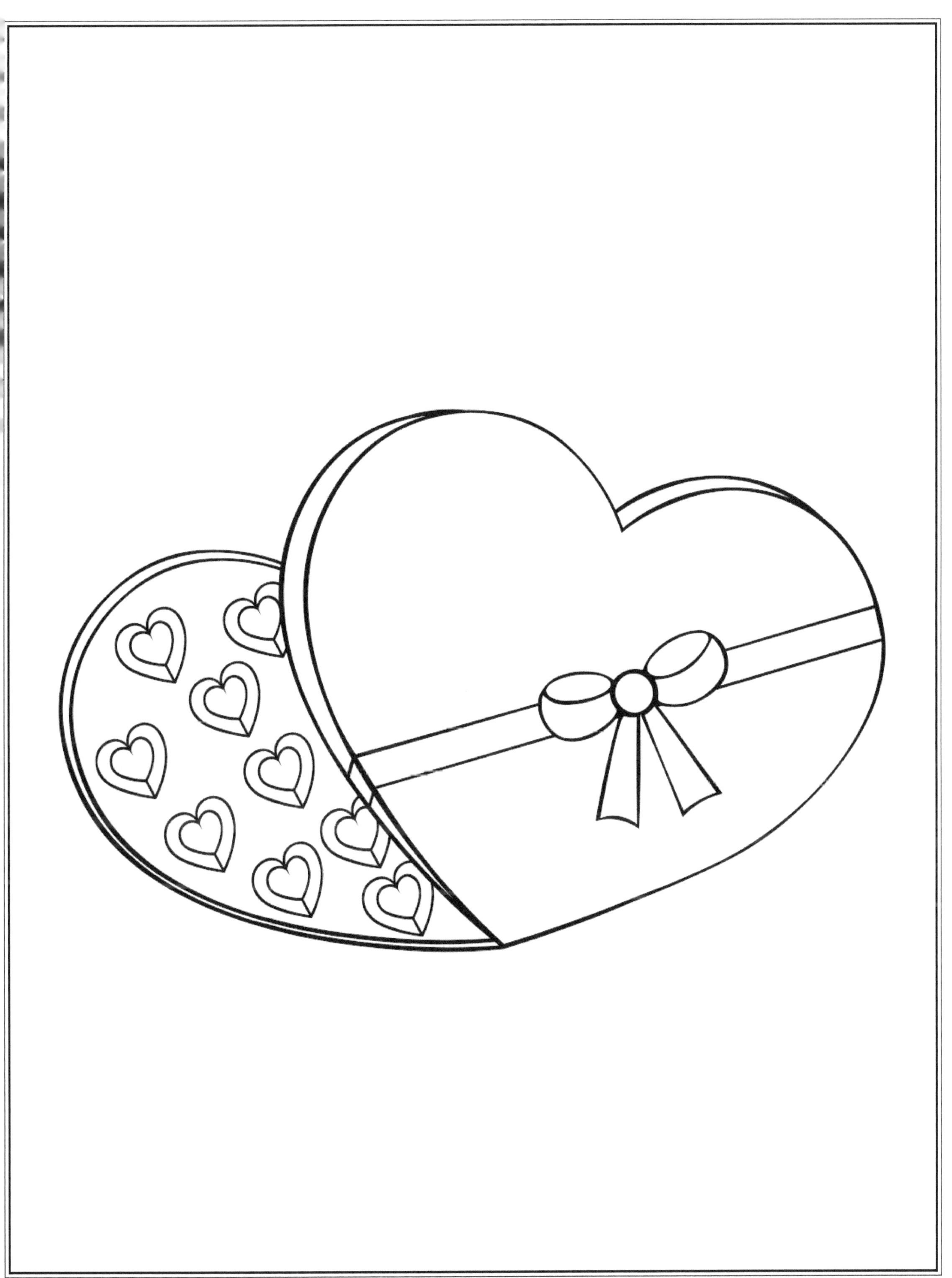

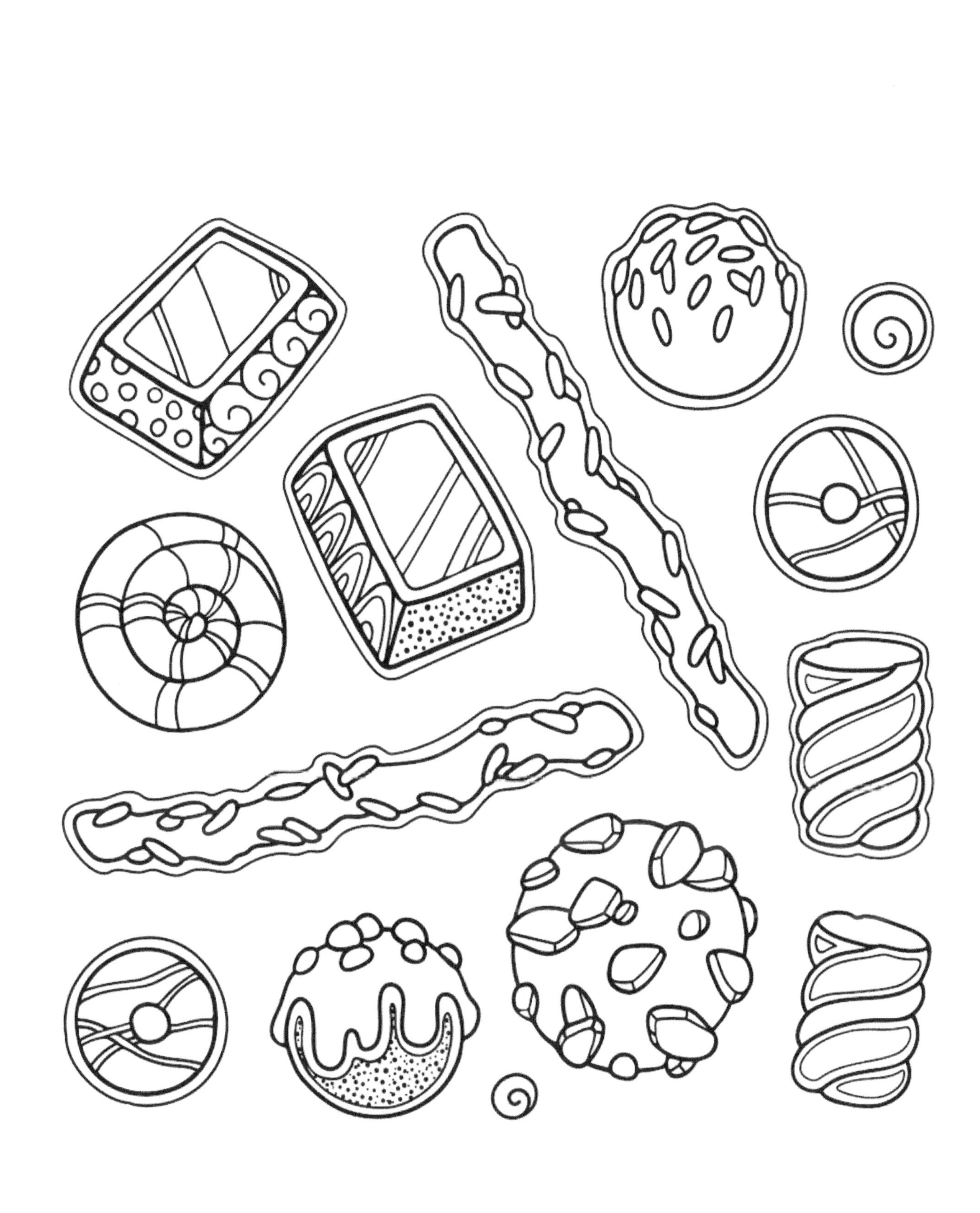

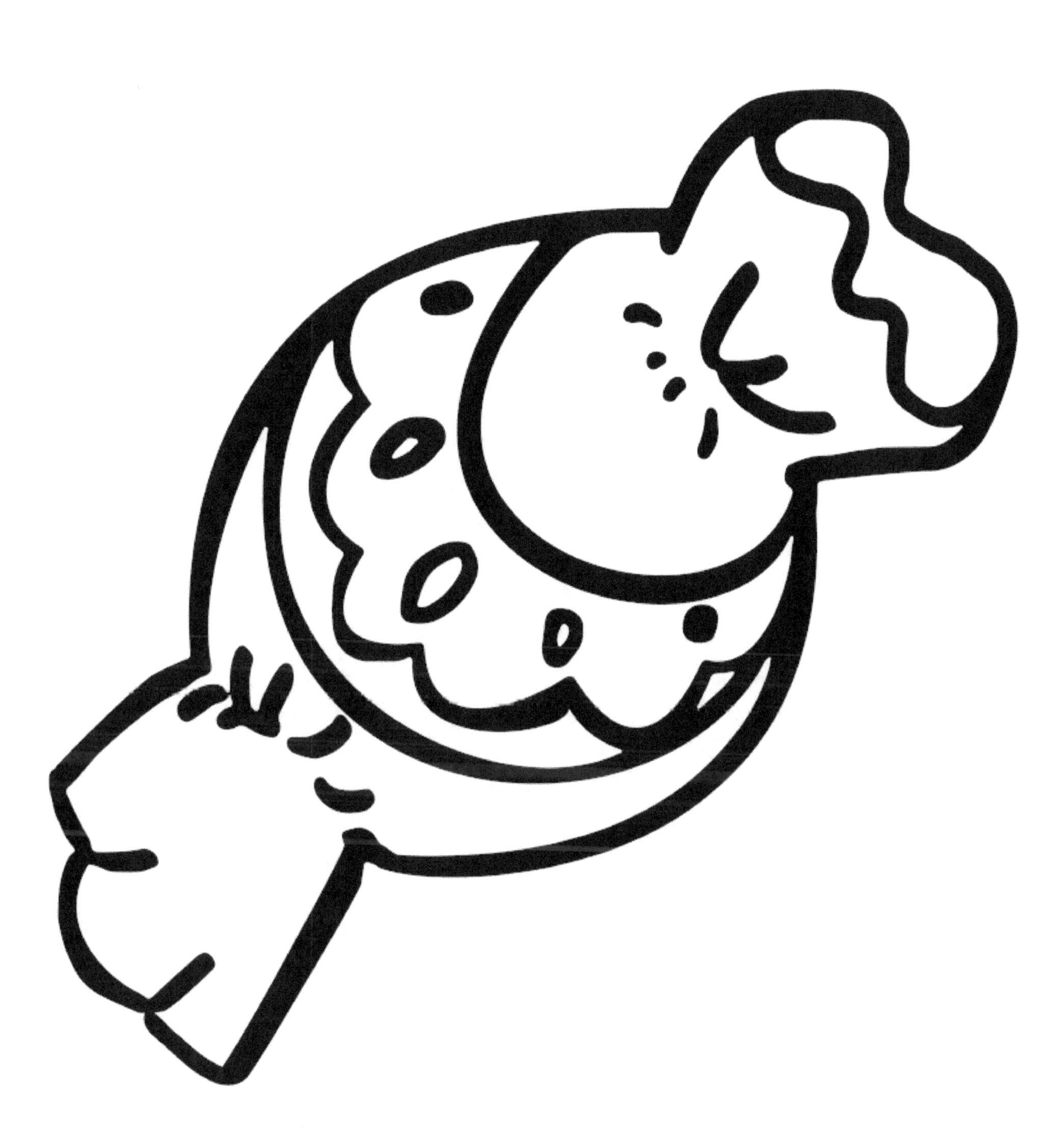

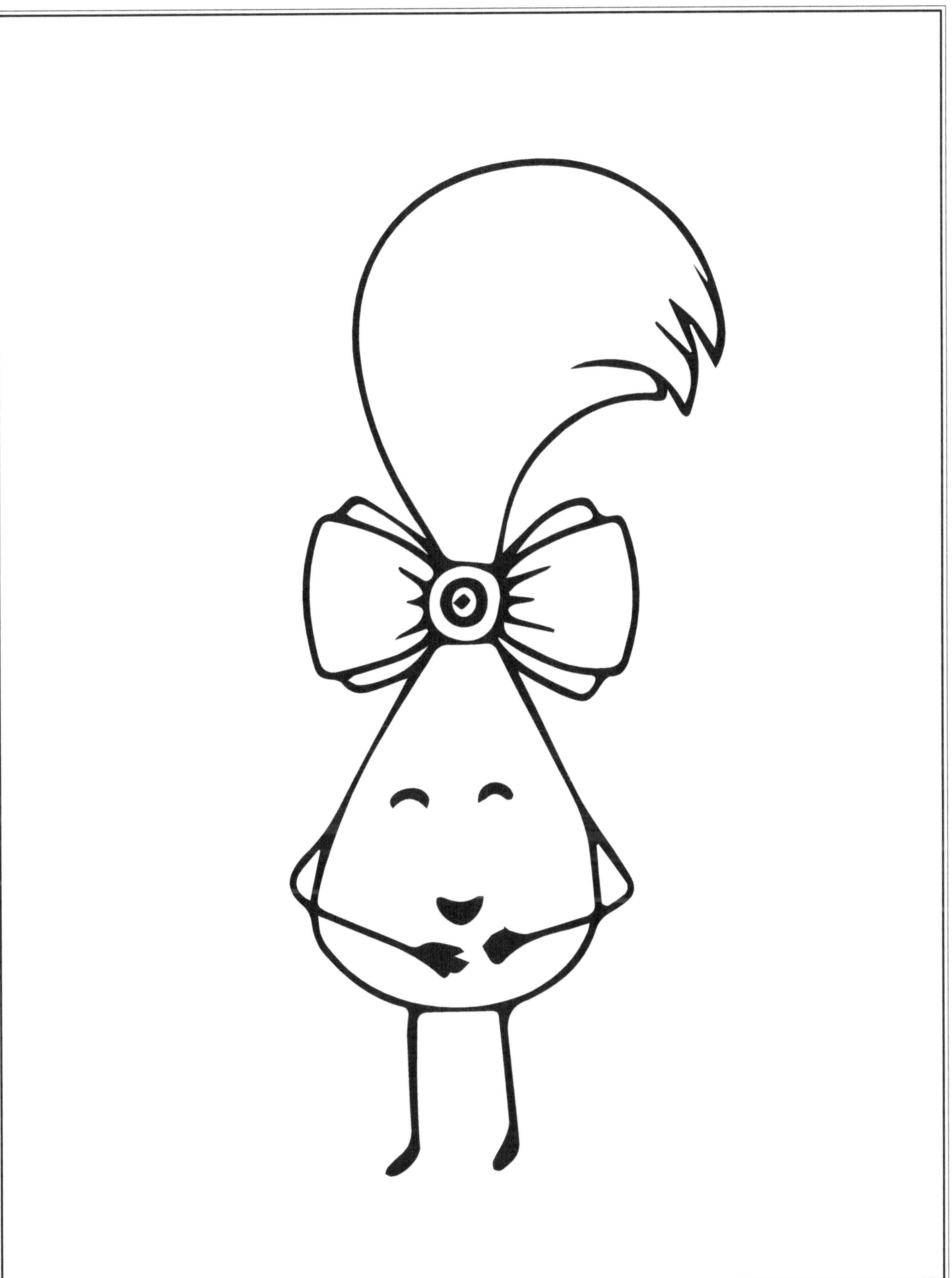

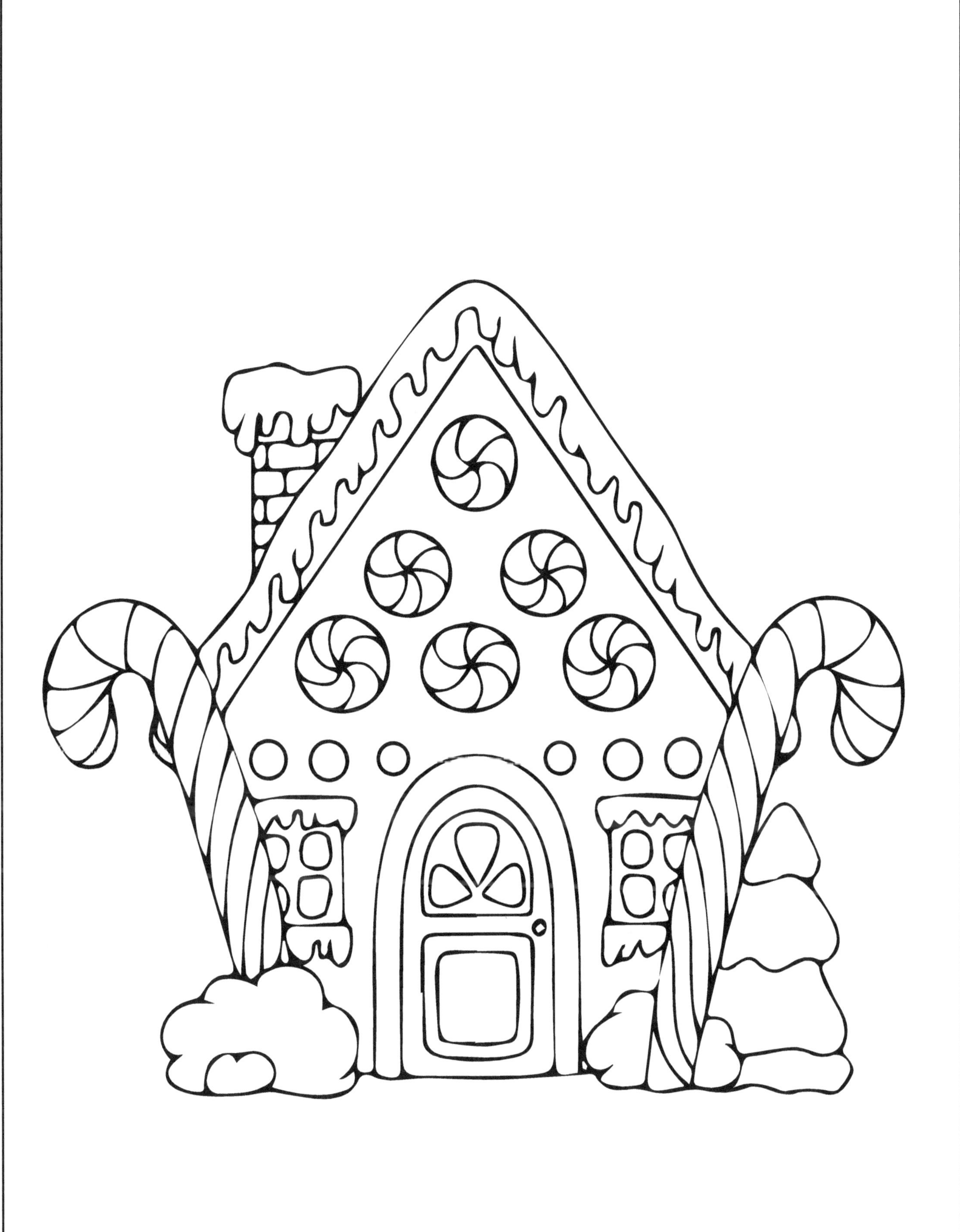

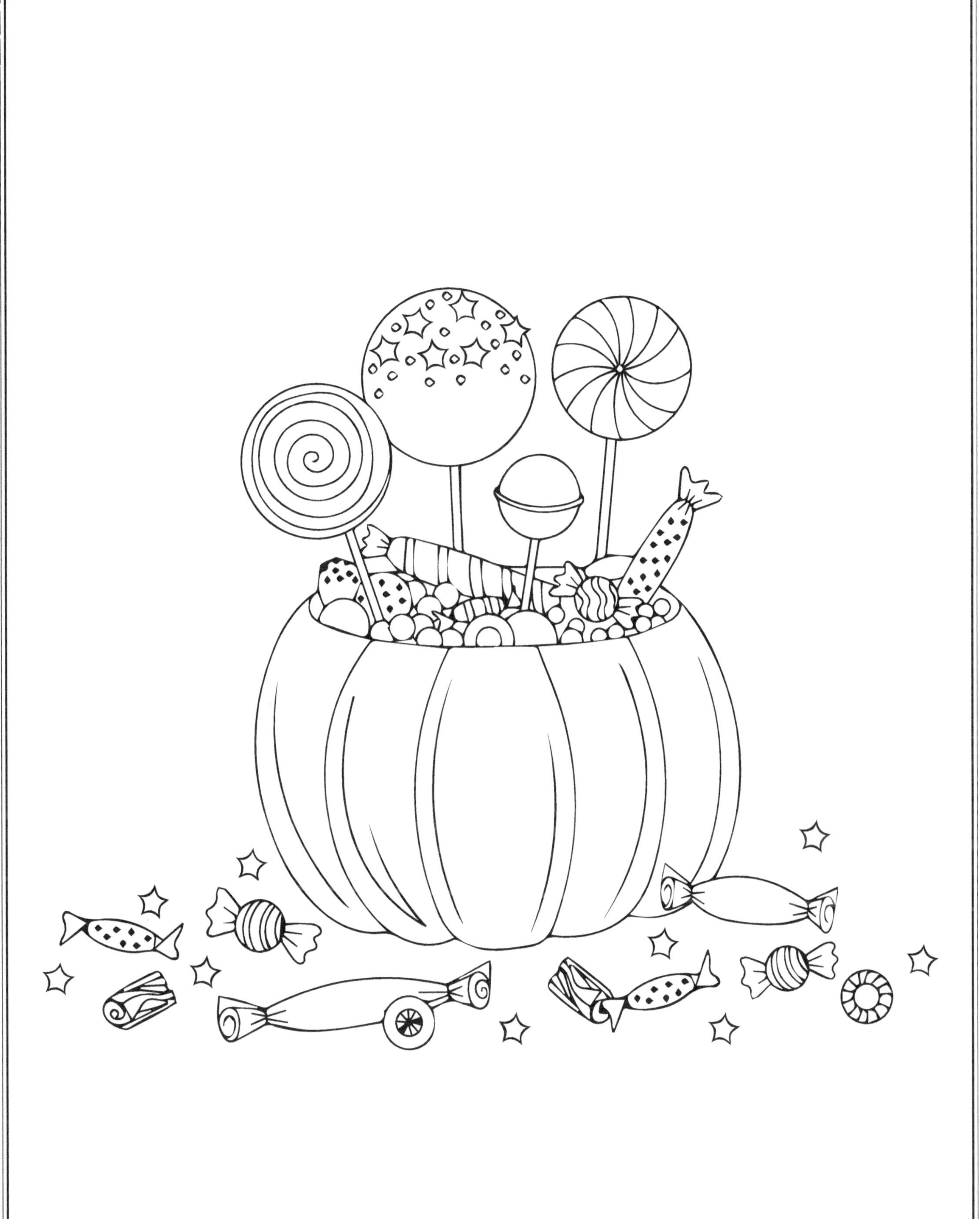

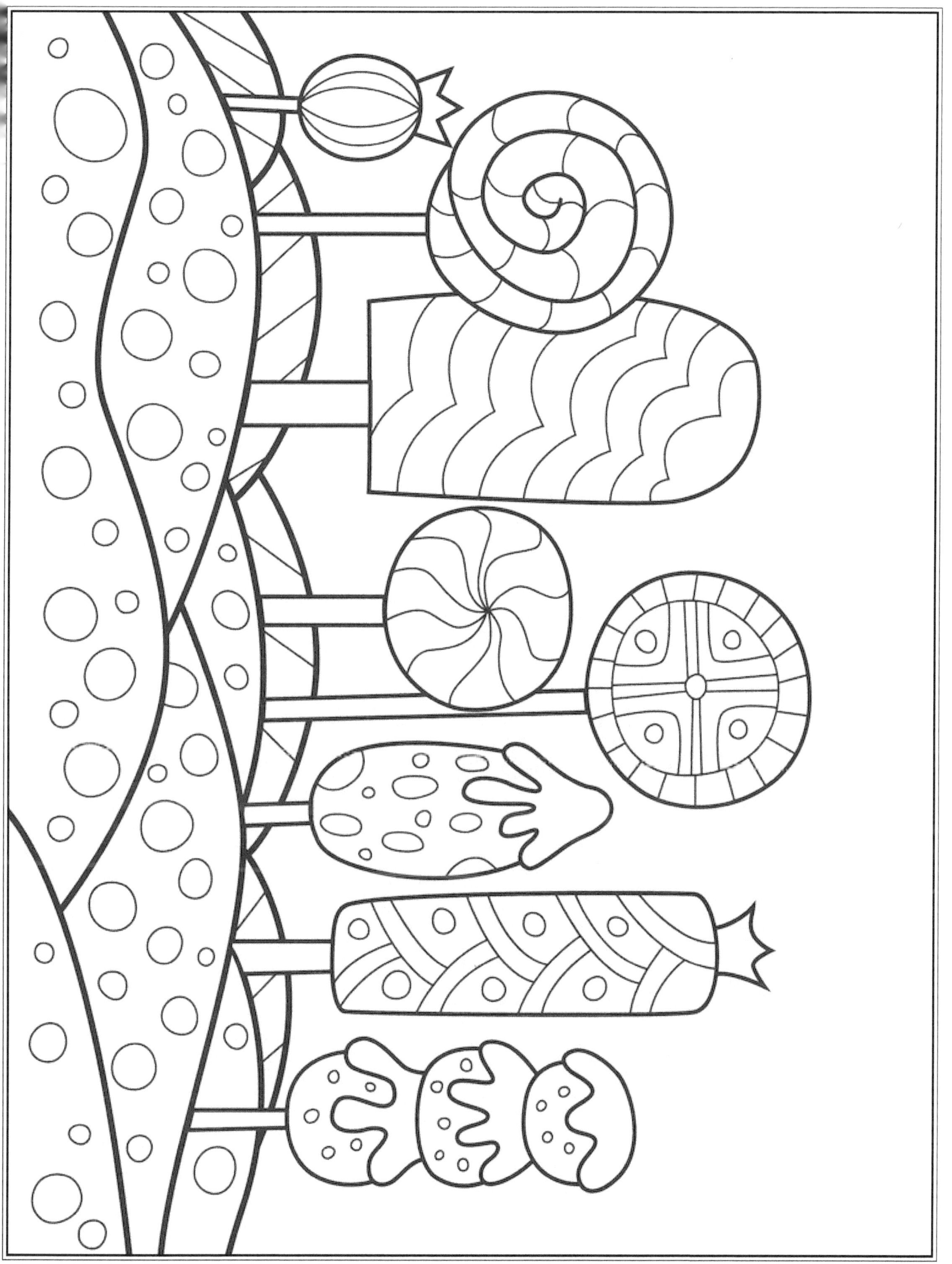

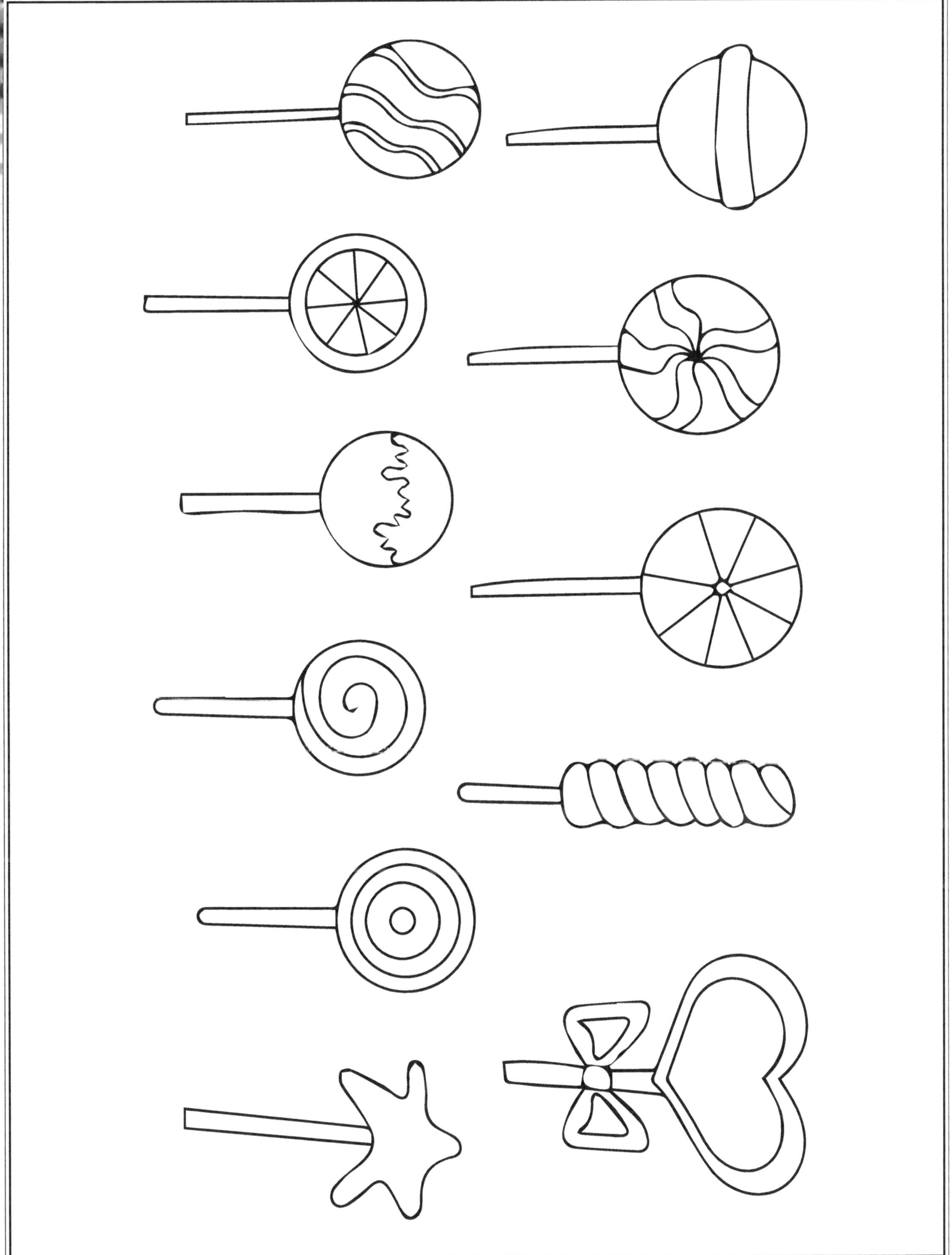

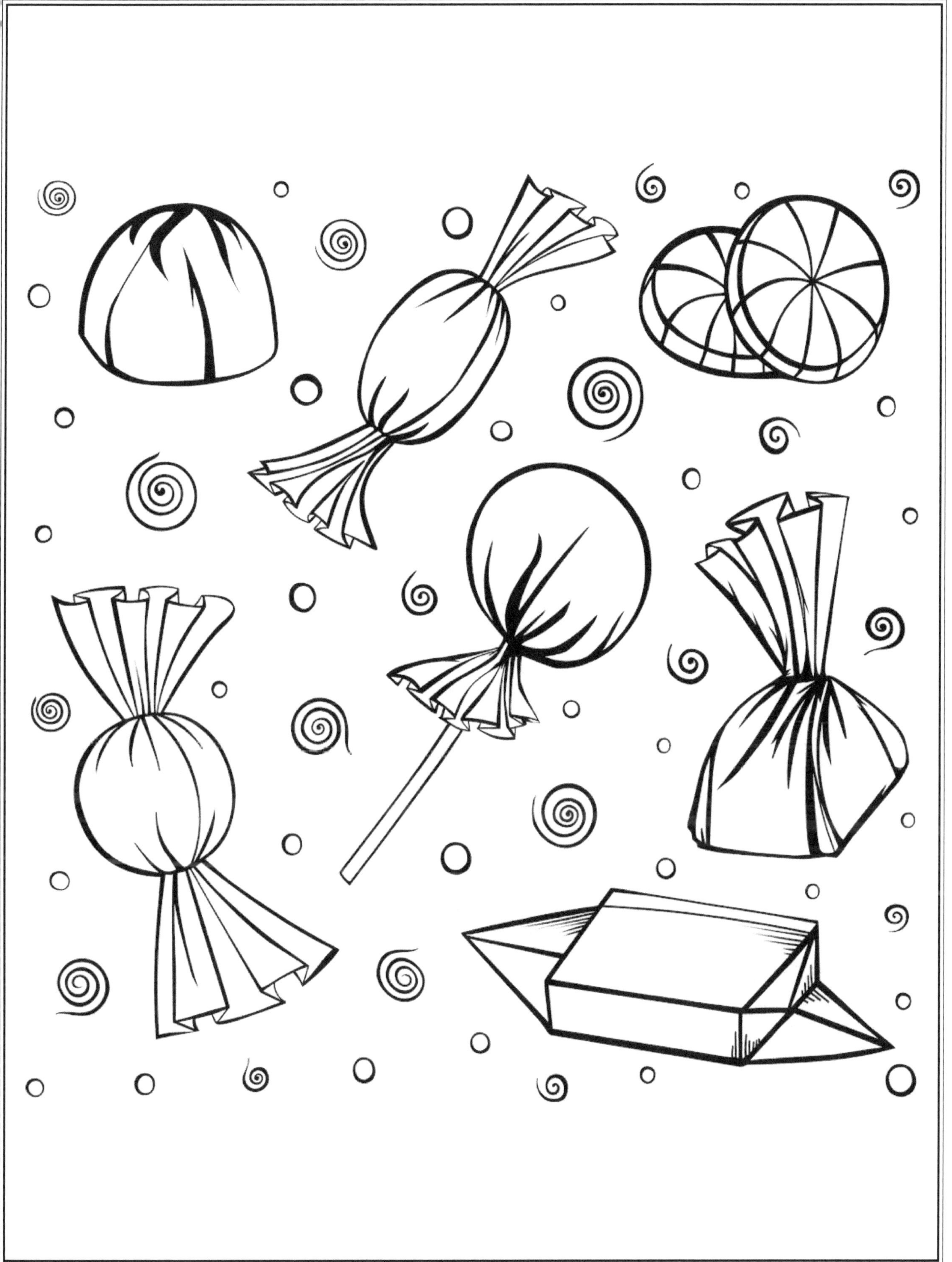

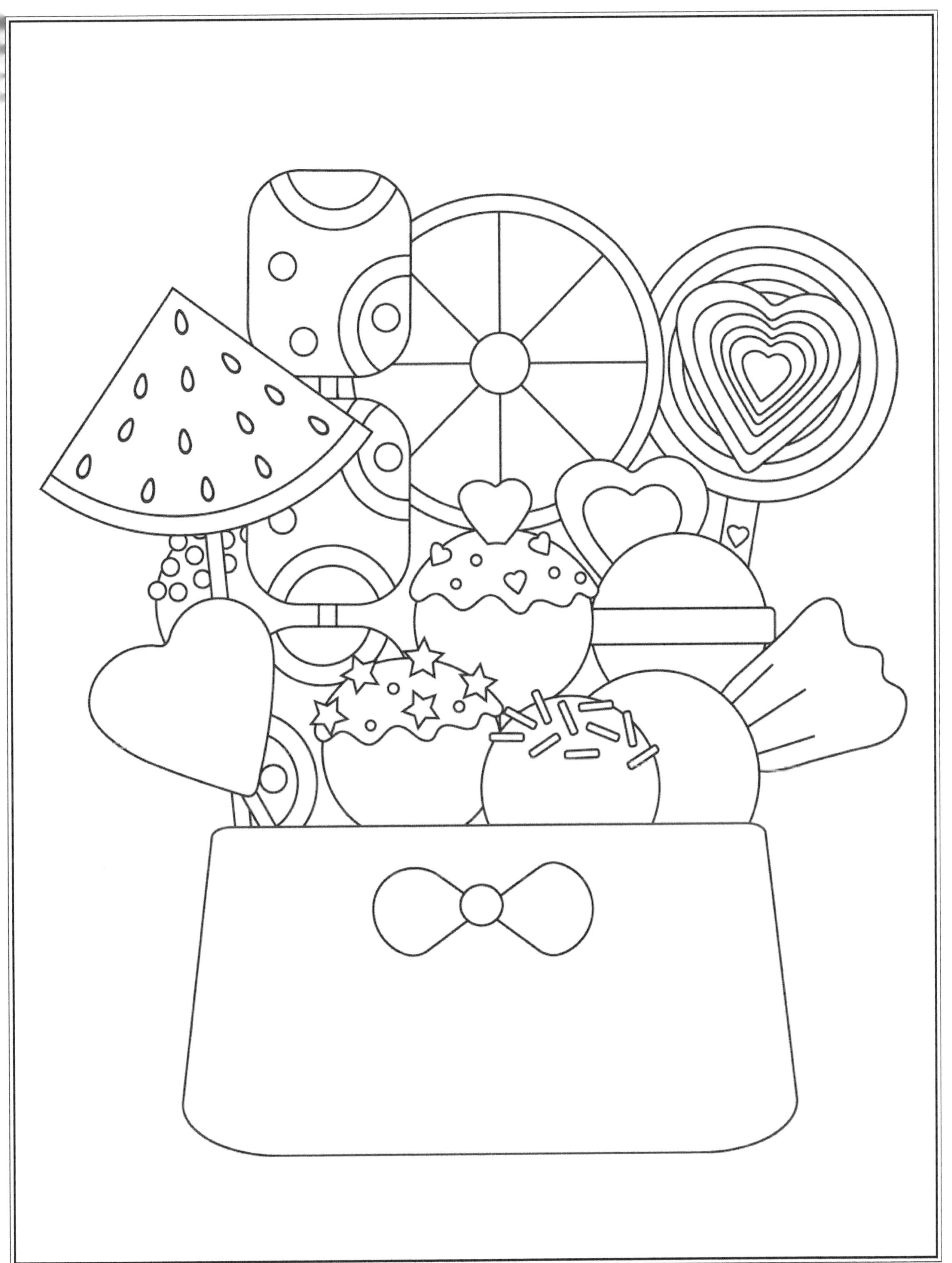

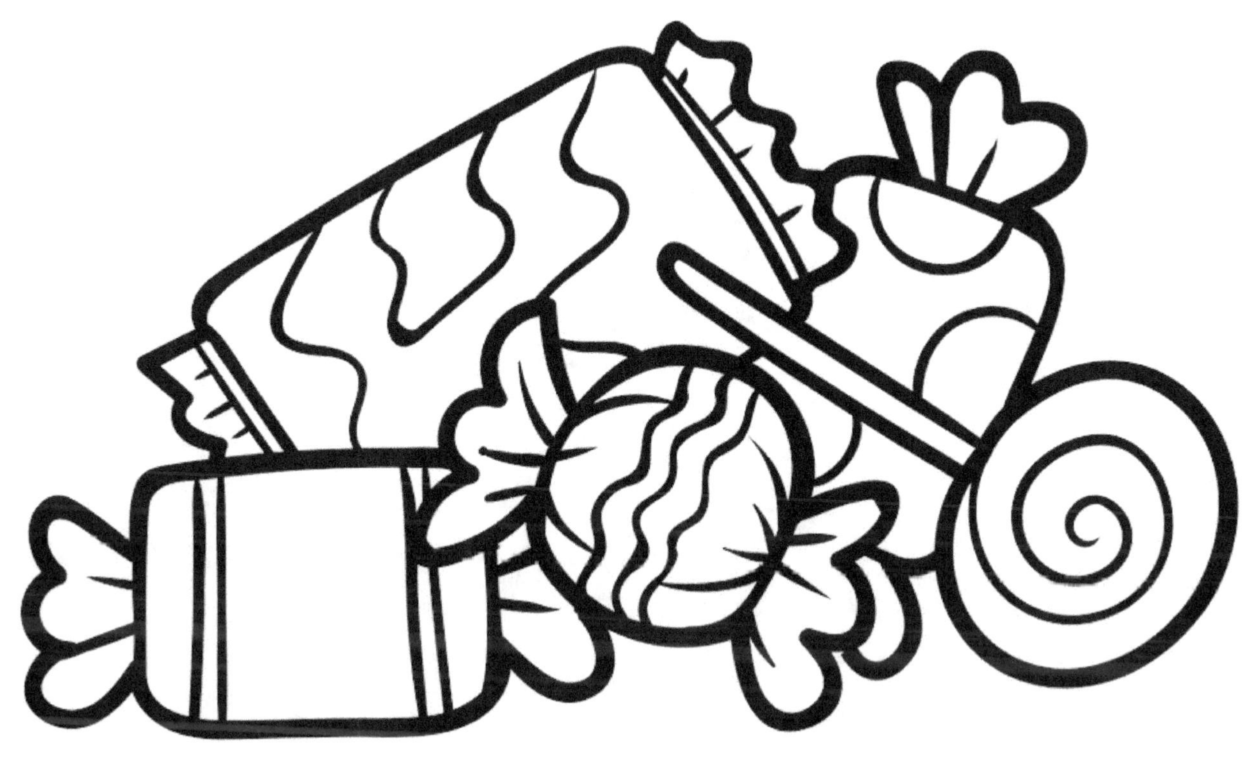